The Courage to Stand Alone

**Conversations with U.G. Krishnamurti
Amsterdam, September 1982**

Transcribed and edited by Ellen Chrystal
from the original audio tapes produced and edited
by Henk Schonewille

NON-DUALITY PRESS

THE COURAGE TO STAND ALONE

This edition published by Non-Duality Press April 2013

My teaching, if that is the word you want to use, has no copyright. You are free to reproduce, distribute, interpret, misinterpret, distort, garble, do what you like, even claim authorship, without my consent or the permission of anybody.

—U.G. Krishnamurti

With gratitude to Louis Brawley, Ellen Chrystal, Sabyasachi Guha, Henk Schonewille and Julie Thayer for making this new edition possible.

Cover photographs by Julie Thayer

NON-DUALITY PRESS | PO Box 2228 | Salisbury | SP2 2GZ
United Kingdom

ISBN: 978-1-908664-28-0

www.non-dualitypress.org

Table of Contents

Foreword

When U.G. invited me in July 1978 to come to Bangalore where he stayed in his friends' house and from where he arranged his Indian travels in those days, my immediate answer was, "Yes Sir, I would like to." At the same time I reminded him of my invitation to him a year before to come to Amsterdam, "Many people there are waiting to see you, Sir." After five years, U.G. finally came to Amsterdam in 1982, and stayed, much to his own surprise, for 21 days in a very nice house offered by some former Rajneeshis. My own house at that time was neither big enough nor otherwise suitable, as, for one thing, Valentine ("my traveling companion," as U.G. called her) was still accompanying U.G. in all his travels.

U.G. fell in love with Amsterdam and its beautiful canals and flowers. The city must have affected him, as could be seen in his clear and powerful talks. Many visitors came to see and talk to him. Among them were psychologists and publishers, spiritual journalists and *sannyasins*, hashish-smoking freaks and 'flower' people. One of them was a well-known poet who had just won an award for "talking without a break for 24 hours." (U.G. silenced him with one sentence!) So, they were quite a mixed bag. Still, I would say they were `ordinary' people.

These tapes held the essence of U.G.'s dialogues in Amsterdam. Fortunately we had installed a tape recorder, and with U.G.'s permission, almost all his talks (some 24 hours of material) were recorded. I did the recording with great enthusiasm and delight. After U.G.'s visit was over, it occurred to me that I could easily produce an audiotape out of that material, primarily for the use of friends. But there was more material than could fit onto one tape, so the effort ended up as the "Give Up" series of three cassettes, of altogether four and a half hours' duration.

I started to edit the U.G. audiotapes around September/ October of 1982, and after the launching I was really surprised that within three weeks I received orders for the tapes from 14 countries. Since then many copies of the "Give Up" tapes found their way around the globe. People called me from Germany, France, Austria, Australia, Italy and so on. Many copies were also made in India.

Every year after that, whenever we met, U.G. remarked, "It seems you have done something tremendous; everyone is praising your tapes, wherever I go." In this printed version of the tapes, we have changed the title to *The Courage to Stand Alone*.

U.G. said to his visitors, "It is nice of you to come here, but you have come to the wrong place—because you want an answer, and you think that my answer will be your answer. But that is not so. I may have found my answer, but that is not your answer. You have to find out for yourself and by yourself the way in which you are functioning in this world, and that will be your answer."

I hope these words of U.G. will help the reader to find "the courage to be on your own; to stand on your two solid feet."

Henk Schonewille
Amsterdam, Holland

Life Discards Everything!

An excerpt from a conversation with Sabyasachi Guha

The search will exemplify both negative and positive aspects, pain and pleasure, and feed into a self-sustaining nature of seeking, glorifying both the pain of suffering and the joy of coincidence that matches the hope of finding the truth. It supplies the energy to continue the very thing that one identified in the first place as the source of the problem. There is really nothing to get! The search has to come to an end.

Q: *It's more like getting stuff out of the way so this thing can just do what it has to.*

Guha: Out of the way means you are not doing anything to get out of the way, you simply know that anything you do is blocking the way. You can't stop thinking about this—that is the unfortunate situation. The viciousness of the cyclic process that causes misery is virtually unrecognizable by the system! As U.G. said, "You will live in hope and die in hope."

Q: *Well this is where they invent all the tricks.*

Guha: Therefore it doesn't work. It produces an apparently achievable, illusory goal. When you have lost your faith in all the tricks, you have to tell yourself there is nothing you can do. The doing question comes because you think you can get something. You can't get anything. Doing is a misnomer;

doing and getting are interlinked. You can get something from somebody, and you know what that is. Then the question comes, what do you do with a personality like U.G.? That's the problem.

Q: *Yeah, what do you do?*

Guha: What do you do? You don't.

Q: *You don't?*

Guha: Of course not, but you are literally focusing on U.G. It has a captivating power. Hindus call it, "*Swayamsampurna,*" which is when an individual is harmoniously connected to the totality of life. It will be noticed, felt, by one who is extremely sensitive. The functionality of a personality like U.G. is the proof of such a possibility. Whatever he was doing it was an expression of life, pure and simple.

Q: *That's why it was so fascinating just to watch him.*

Guha: Yes, because that is life. Life never copies. That's what he was trying to show all the time. His negation had a fundamental necessity; he was totally denying everybody's imagination about a behavior that they were expecting from him. That didn't mean that he would do some odd thing on the street or tell somebody something that was not necessary. He knew... yet he was denying! There is something inside and when it moves powerfully that movement is infinitely more important than satisfying people's expectations. Those ideas are based on the cultural background and the image-making aspect of the individual mind.

People who came to talk to U.G. had various ideas about what it would be like to meet a realized person, a *brahmajnani,* or *atmajnani,* who had achieved *nirvana* or

4

enlightenment. These are very loaded words and for centuries people tried to understand and experiment with their functionality. The moment you utter those terms, depending on your cultural background and conditioning, there are feelings and expectations! This was our *numero uno* intentionality because it signaled the end of all problems. These dynamics created the stage on which one person acts like a god and others are being helped by that enlightened one! People don't know to what extent they are puppets of the culture. When we confront a personality like U.G., whose very existence is an order in the space of life, we sense our imaginary order is an imposition and disturbance, so we confront abnegation. He was so confirmed from within that he knew very well it was useless to satisfy the expectation of behavior from a person's fictitious and illusory knowledge. He would mock our concepts of purity and holiness. This is why he often used vulgar words, to shatter that image.

Q: *He could say anything he wanted.*

Guha: Yes, he would joyfully say he peed on Ganesha's idol and shat on Ramana Maharshi's picture.

Q: *What is it he said in the Yercaud talks? "You're listening to me because you think what I am saying is what those people said before, and it's not."*

Guha: We want to preserve our past glory and icons, but U.G. was an iconoclast. There is an undeniable effect of what U.G. stands for. There was a time when I used to feel that the sheer luminescence of U.G. was going to make me blind, and some other time the incandescence of that heat was going to make me faint. I began to observe that other people were also physically responding to U.G.'s energy. Julie was the supreme example of "U.G. cooking." I used to think that her brain cells would be thoroughly reorganized —I called it radioactive exposure, which cooks silently. He was like a radioactive source. If you are exposed to it, you don't know it but you're burning inside—your cells are getting cooked—of course the meaning of the word "exposed" is very important.

That's what I was literally feeling. How would I compare these things? The references were so uncommon and extraordinary that I had to use these strange scientific examples. Whatever I was conveying was not what it was—I realized that fact every time I made reference to it. Yet we are forced to talk! This is one of the reasons that my way of expressing it is always different, looking for an example to give a hint or sense of the source of my physical response and the feelings generated from it.

I used to tell people, "Look, there is nothing you can do. All you have to look for is the day you are going to fall in love with this guy." That's it. You don't need anything else. Why? Falling in love means you want to spend more time with the person. That's the meaning, right? Nothing is better than a lover's company, no matter how torturous. It's the only way you can withstand the pain, that's the equation.

Q: *That's the equation. It may sound embarrassing, but it's a fact.*

Guha: You are like a puppy! You are mine, I am yours, take everything I have! So, if that happens, it means you have him inside your unconscious brain! It appeared to me that U.G. was really conveying that to me.

One day we were in a store, U.G., Julie and I. We were moving around, looking for something that was not available. At that time my whole being was a question mark and U.G. was constantly hammering the point that no answer could end the questioning mechanism. One cannot force such a thing into operation because the one who forces is the major problem, so the frustrated me, the hungry me, trying to understand every gem that dropped from his tongue, staring enviously at his every move, wanted to kneel down and beg for an answer, so that this system would no longer be tortured by this scientific beast that wants to know. After some time we came to an aisle, my whole being was nothing but questions. I was like a zombie moving around him, and suddenly he turned and looked at me as if to say, "Ask anything you want." I made a gesture like, "Tell me what I can do." Then he immediately pointed his finger towards a poster on the wall. I literally froze and asked him, "Are you pointing to that one?" He answered in no uncertain terms, "Yes!" The poster read: "LOVE IS THE ONLY WAY." Okay! He didn't stop there. He said to me, "Show it to your sissy." Julie was looking at something else. I just jumped at her, and literally pulled her to show her the poster. In the meantime, U.G. almost vanished, probably because he knew she would flip and buy the whole store to commemorate such an event. That was Julie …

Another day I was standing in Julie's living room at 1 West 64th Street, talking to U.G. She was cooking in the kitchen and he was in a great mood, laughing and joking. He used to do that more and more as my vacation days would approach their end. I said, "Sir, I have to go home." He responded, "Where is your home?" I literally hugged him, and squeezed him hard. He didn't take my hands off or move away; instead he called Julie and said, "Hey, hey, look what this fellow is doing!" She was out of her mind when I told her what U.G. had just said that caused my exuberance. He was a living system that was, as he used to say, "stimulus and response." During that period I would do anything just to stay with him. I feel he sensed what was going on with me, and I was going through hell. The pulverizing attraction of U.G. was on one side and the rest of the justification process that my self-consciousness was dealing with opposed it on the other. It was a constant, agonizing struggle.

This is a story I must tell you. The president of Sri Ram Chandra Mission where I had been practicing Raja Yoga before I met U.G. came to know that I had stopped coming to *satsang* and he was very unhappy about it. He asked the other local devotees somehow to bring me back to the mission. At that time almost all my friends were in that mission, so everyone started enquiring because I had completely stopped meditation for many months. It was impossible to tell them that the promised goal itself is an illusion. Anyway the "Master" finally came to New York and he asked my friends to tell me to give him a call and if necessary he would give me a special "sitting." This man had at least 5,000 disciples in the US and Europe alone, all who were dying for his company. I told my friends that I had no interest in this kind of game anymore so just "fugetaboutit!" They told me he was going to call me.

During this time, I used to call U.G. almost every day. In the beginning of these commotions I didn't mention anything to him. As soon as it came to this point, I thought of discussing this matter with him, but suddenly U.G. was no longer available. It was so weird; this man with whom I had been talking on a daily basis was suddenly avoiding me at that critical juncture.

The president of the mission called me towards the end of his stay in the New York area. I told him that what I had been practicing with him was just an idea and I was no longer interested in it, consequently the activity of the mission was finding no feedback in me. He said that this was a "good state" and I should continue. I told him that, unless I came to know for myself that it was a good state and that my continuation was important, I would do nothing further. At this point he got angry. He warned me, "You know there are people who made this kind of mistake and later, after

8

realizing it, came and fell at my feet, and asked me to forgive them for their mistake. I don't want this to happen to you." Suddenly something twisted in me, a movement in the gut, and I told him, "I would rather die than turn back." That was the end of that chapter of my life.

U.G. came to New York about a month after that. I was excited to see him. He refused to stay in Julie's apartment this time, I thought he was being playful and would change his mind, but he meant it. There was no room at the Southgate where he had often stayed, so he ended up at the Hotel Iroquois. I came there in the early morning and was happy beyond description. He started making breakfast for the two of us. The oatmeal was overflowing when he poured heavy cream on it and I commented, "Sir, it is like your love, no vessel can contain it." He reacted almost violently and told me with a force that I didn't realize was possible, "Love is a filthy word!" I couldn't utter anything, and mechanically finished my breakfast.

Then I told him what had happened during the time I couldn't reach him by phone, that I just couldn't find even an iota of interest in me to go and meet that person. I was enquiring honestly, I wanted to find out why I had had that struggle about meeting the head of the mission, and why I had had difficulty explaining to my friends my unwillingness to meet him. One of my closest friends, someone whom I had introduced to U.G. on previous visits and whose uncle was a close friend of U.G.'s in India, had wanted to know what was wrong in discussing spiritual matters with the master of that mission.

U.G. kept quiet and just listened, and when I finished, he looked at my face with a strange, distant, vacant expression as if no one was there and he was not addressing anyone, and said, "If you had gone there, you would have lost everything." I almost flipped. I mean I had been just this close to seeing that man, because every single friend of mine

9

was asking me to go. U.G.'s comment was like a stab in my heart, truly! It shattered my entire existence. He was deadly serious. That would have been a miscarriage, I would have produced a dead baby; it felt like that.

This incident rotated in my head for months. I couldn't tell this to anybody. I knew something was going on in my physical existence but logically U.G.'s comment seemed to be the antithesis of his own philosophy. Things he said had meaning to a particular person in a particular context, it may not have any significance later or to another person. That's the only story we can tell. The fact always revealed to me was that there were things he took care of personally, that were for your own wellbeing, with no sentimentality, no possessiveness. It seems now as if he was taking a big risk of being misunderstood! Really! I mean, those words will always live with me. My seeking ended, something was growing inside me, and I had to look after it! There is nothing to look for outside myself anymore. I don't need anything from anybody; I don't need any confirmation or justification. All I need is money to survive in this man-made world. Money is oxygen in social dynamics, you need it to breathe. You need money to live. Period. To live sanely and intelligently in this world you need decent food, clothing and shelter. I don't want to live like a bum, but that doesn't mean that I am critical of people who do. If you have some talent, why shouldn't you use it to get what you need to get according to your wisdom? Don't make a virtue of failure, and if you have means you are lucky, that's all. No one can tell an adult individual what he needs.

I will tell you another incident. At the time when U.G. fell, and you were taking care of him in his underground studio in Gstaad, Bob was also there interviewing people. He wanted to make a documentary about how people were being affected by U.G. He asked me for an interview, and I said, "Forget it."

I have so many personal anecdotes of my own which kind of deify U.G., and I really don't want to do that. He is inside me; if there is something real they will know about him by seeing how I function, what he made of me. I don't worship him, and I don't want to sell him in the marketplace and use him for my own self-aggrandizement, protection and fear, it's not like that. This is important to me. I was also very deeply aware that too much discussing about the physical aspects would make me sound like I'm trying to copy him. Describing things as they are was the only thing I was feeling gutsy about because it didn't require any reference. U.G. friends didn't like to hear that from me, there was a general consensus that only U.G. could talk like that. I couldn't sit like that and talk, it's not my way. I wanted to go into detail and the implications, but I didn't do that in the beginning.

One day we were all sitting around U.G., and Bob told U.G. that he was interviewing everybody, but Guha refused to be interviewed. And I said, "Holy shit." No offense, but I didn't realize that he was going to put me on the cross like that. And U.G. was so sweet, didn't enquire what happened or ask me anything, but after barely five minutes, he suddenly brought up this energy topic, you know, "America's energy is in Guha's hands," the usual stuff...

Q: *The superconductivity.*

Guha: Superconductivity, the energy business.* I had no say in the matter but Larry wanted to carry on the conversation with U.G. because he always wanted to engage him so that he could hear some more things. "So Guha tell me, what will happen if suddenly there is a vacuum (meaning U.G.

---

*Guha is a physicist and at that time he was working at Rutgers University doing research in the field of superconductivity.

is not there, you know), what will happen?" I said, "Larry, don't worry about others, don't worry about what will happen to anybody. If you can handle this guy in this life, I guarantee you, if you are successful in handling this man, come close to this man, once you've dealt with this man, you will never, ever, ever in this birth need anybody again for that purpose."

U.G. said, "Bob, that's your interview!" He added, "If you don't know this by now, you will never know it." That was the thing, like, there is nothing to know, there is something that you have tested, and the validity is functioning inside you, it is a life-abiding experience. If you learn swimming, you just know, you don't think about it, it's part of you. The evidence of the functionality in you is all that matters; it gives you the courage to stand on your own two feet.

Introduction

by Julie Thayer

I met U.G. Krishnamurti for the first time in May 1989, in Seaside, California at the home of a philosophy professor, Narayana Moorty. My first impression was of a small, graceful, fluid man with a disarming way about him, utterly lacking in pretense or guile. A power emanated from him that seemed to turn my brain to slush. When he spoke I heard him as if from a great distance. Later, when I said I was from New York, he told me that it was his favorite city. He said he particularly liked the intense energy around Times Square.

I thought, "I don't want to leave this man."

Two days later I went to see U.G. again in Mill Valley with four fellow disciples of a spiritual teacher I had been associated with for about a year. I found him sitting in a dimly lit, tiny room in the "Crow's Nest," the home of a friend. He was surprisingly passive, inert. We sat across from him in a strange silence, waiting for a dialogue, but none was forthcoming. It seemed the impasse might go on indefinitely, it was somewhat awkward. It wasn't until I asked a question, "U.G., is it necessary to surrender to a guru?", that he roused himself and spoke. "What are you surrendering?" he asked intently. "Just your self-reliance."

I was hooked.

We talked some more, and after awhile, U.G. asked, "Isn't that enough?" We said goodbye, left him and stood in the street outside the Crow's Nest conferring with each other and, astonishingly, we found that each of us realized at the same moment we were finished with our teacher! I had been forbidden to drive for the last six months or so, it was a *sadhana* of some sort given by my now ex-guru, and when one of my friends asked if I wanted to drive home, I said, "Yes, I do, absolutely!" and I hopped into the driver's seat. It was a heady and liberating moment.

I saw U.G. several more times before he left California, then returned to the East Coast. Subsequently I telephoned him in Switzerland and invited him to stay in my apartment if and when he came to New York. A few months later, on my 49th birthday, he took me up on it! Strangely, it did not strike me as unusual that he would arrive at my door with his small bag and minimal possessions and simply move in with someone he barely knew. In fact there was something about him that made me feel I had known him my whole life.

During that visit, U.G. invited me to travel around the world with him, taking photos and videos. It was the beginning of a long, challenging, and ultimately astonishing relationship for me, the single most crucial encounter of my life.

Seven years after my first meeting with U.G., and sixteen years ago, Autonomedia, an anarchist press in Brooklyn, published this book, *The Courage to Stand Alone*. During that time Ellen Chrystal and I made countless visits to their warehouse in Williamsburg, which had been recently raided by the FBI! We made arrangements there for the design and distribution of the book and it felt like the perfect vehicle for U.G.'s views. He would say, "Anarchy is a state of *being*, not doing!", and he seemed pleased by our choice of publishers.

Time has passed, and with it there have been several Indian editions and numerous translations of *The Courage to Stand Alone*. U.G. himself has passed on. Writing about him is always somewhat daunting. One feels a certain inadequacy; still, on the eve of the publication of this newest

14

edition, I find myself moved to reflect on this man's life, and the impact he has had on my own.

For almost twenty years UG's presence in my life was critical, glorious, painful... always, as he put it, "walking the razor's edge," with no margin for error. He would say, "If you want one thing, you will get it, if you want two things, ten things, forget about it. As long as there is a sense of obligation to others, and to 'things', you cannot be here." If everything mankind has thought, felt and experienced was wiped out of his system in 1967 when he had his "calamity," how on earth could I expect to satisfy cultural pressure and expectations and at the same time strike out independently?

Someone told me recently that in his view U.G. was not "there," there was no U.G. there, as if his apparent being was an illusion, that there was no U.G. there to be disappointed or pleased. My experience of him was very different. To me he was eminently sensitive and responsive, he felt *everything*, more than we could imagine. The difference is that nothing stayed with him; he didn't and couldn't hold onto things. For him every moment was a rebirth, a fresh take, with no carryover. *We* carry things over, exhaustingly, compulsively—and perhaps those lingering sentiments triggered the epic, famous blasting responses from him.

We can talk forever about how U.G. functioned, but nobody knows for sure since our experience of him could only be subjective. His long-time landlord in Gstaad, Switzerland, the late Mr. Grossmann, said to me one night in 1997, "People don't understand or appreciate U.G., they come to him with forks to drink soup."

Still, certain things stand out. Sitting in the car outside Fairway Market in New York, overlooking the Hudson River, U.G. was asked, "What should one *do*?" His answer, simply put, was *"Essen, trinken und schlafen."* Eat, drink and sleep.

"Nothing else?" Nothing else.

That was his message... or one of them. There is no need, indeed no room, in the efficiently functioning system for anything else. On my first trip to Bangalore with him in 1990, someone asked about the "path." His answer, "Total surrender... not to anyone, but to whatever is happening." The clarity of his answers continues to astonish, reverberate, shatter the mind.

U.G. practiced what he preached, living in a kind of radical simplicity, cutting through the annals and byways of convention and offering a pared-down, cut to the chase approach to life, a glimpse of a reality few come into, yet there for everyone, the bottom line of human existence. Having the *courage to stand alone* means to live as nature intended, respecting the body and its innate intelligence, deferring to its "order," not to the delusional order of the mind, the "squatter," that constitutes "us," without aspiring to any concepts of "how to live," liberation or enlightenment. To have wants and needs on an equal plane, not taking the advice of therapists, self-help peddlers and holy men, but standing alone apart from the cultural do's and don'ts of family and society. Leaving it all alone, yet not being in conflict with any of it, just ignoring certain pressures.

"If you are freed from the burden of the entire past of mankind, then what is left there is the courage."

U.G. could not be manipulated by anyone or anything, yet he was "doing" for others all the time, on *his* terms—doing what life dictated, devoid of guilt and compulsions. Nothing could strike a discordant note in him; he didn't function that way. Once I told him I "loved" him, and he answered, "I would never say I love you, but I would do anything for you." Yet in a cheap discount store (the kind of place he loved) on the Upper West Side of New York, he pointed to a poster on the wall that said, "LOVE IS THE ONLY WAY." "Show that to your sissy," he said of me, to our mutual friend Guha.

16

"Attraction is the *action*," he would say.

"I negate the first statement with the second, and negate the second statement with the third! The fourth negates all three." Walking by a construction site in the streets of Melbourne he said to me, "That jackhammer *is* the Silence." He went on to say that sound could stop thinking in its tracks, for a moment or two. Or, as the train roared by his house in Gstaad, he would point to it and say, "*That* is your teacher."

His message and being were disarmingly simple and incredibly forceful. There was enormous power in that frail human body, and he was eminently practical in the execution of his life. The scriptures of India describe a *brahmajnani* like U.G. as a "monster, madman, and a child." From one moment to the next he was all of these things, childlike and impossibly difficult, a philosopher of the highest order, unique, brilliant, unpredictable but predictably disarming, powerful and perceptive.

Once someone said to me, "You being you, it's astonishing that you had the discrimination to fall for U.G." That was just my great luck, a fluke of fate. Discrimination, if that's what it is, is the aspiration to stand alone, (*noting that nothing else one has done in one's life has had any recognizable lasting effect, nothing has helped*) ... because that is what U.G. did and what he represented to me. He needed no confirmation from anyone, no approval, he just lived as he lived, as he saw fit, traveling on his own until age caught up with him, carrying his own 5 kilo suitcase with all his earthly possessions, cooking his oatmeal every morning, wherever he was on the planet, often with the help of the tiny portable kitchen he carried with him for years. His door was always open to whoever came by to talk, no one ever ran things for him, or stood in the way of anyone else having access to him—that was emphatically "not allowed!!"

Once I asked him to teach me how to pack like he did, with such expertise. "It's easier to teach enlightenment," he said, and added, "and enlightenment doesn't exist!"

When U.G. could no longer take care of his own needs, move as he wished, he refused to depend on the intervention of the medical profession or the help of anybody. He just gracefully passed away. He never compromised the integrity of his own words until his last breath.

U.G.'s presence and his words deeply influenced innumerable people. He touched a chord that had surely never resonated before. Now, after his death, we see and hear that effect extending itself exponentially, thanks to the internet and more and more books. Perhaps his impact is even more powerful for those who never met him in person, though I believe all of us who lived with or near him, traveled with him, merged their lives with his are fortunate beyond belief. If his influence could help people stand on their own without getting lured into easy cures and offers from religious figures and gurus of something that simply does not exist (enlightenment, salvation, permanent happiness), dragging humanity out of the emperor's new clothes world it lives in, how great it would be!!!

"I don't know what happiness is, therefore I can never be unhappy!" He couldn't be fit into a religious context—it just couldn't be done. U.G. used to recite one of his favorite Sanskrit lines from the Upanishads, when people would ask him about "that state" …

> "Na pravachanena na medhaya, na bahunasrutena na karmanye, na prajaya na dhanena, tyagenaike amrutatwa manasaha." Not through scripture, not through intellect, not by repeated listening, not through any work (karma yoga), not through heredity (lineage) and not through money…only through total renunciation can one reach the eternal state of mind.

18

U.G. said you have to "give up" everything that you are doing to get whatever you are trying to get. "But," he would then say, "there is nothing to get!" More and more these days, I feel U.G.'s presence and his face floats before me, his words echo in my mind ... "You are not in a position to agree or disagree with anything I say. Take it or leave it."

I reflect on him and I realize now how right he was about things and how little I understood when I was with him. My neurotic and frivolous thinking took me away again and again—and again and again he would welcome me back, and offer his wisdom and protection and another start. He wanted nothing from any of us, yet offered the only pointers that could help us, pointers so incredibly difficult to implement. U.G. was the person who stood by me for eighteen years through thick and thin, almost a third of my adult life, who blasted me to help me, who never compromised, never made things easy, because he knew it wouldn't change things to give in to ignorance, neurosis, folly.

When I sometimes feel a bit desperate about his absence, I can hear his voice, "You are not *that* desperate, Madam!" He always said the hope is in the hopelessness. To heal a broken heart you must break it more.

A person who is truly independent of any authority or any idea has the courage to stand alone.

That was U.G.

Julie Thayer
New York 2012

Part I

You Don't Have To Do A Thing

Q: *U.G., do you agree with me that you live in a frictionless state?*

U.G.: Not in conflict with the society—this is the only reality I have, the world as it is today. The ultimate reality that man has invented has absolutely no relationship whatsoever with the reality of this world. As long as you are seeking, searching, and wanting to understand that reality, which you call "ultimate reality" or call it by whatever name you like, so long it will not be possible for you to come to terms with the reality of the world exactly the way it is. So, anything you do to escape from the reality of this world will make it difficult for you to live in harmony with the things around you.

We have an idea of harmony. How to live at peace with yourself—that's an idea. But already, there is an extraordinary peace that is there. What makes it difficult for you to live at peace with yourself is the creation of what you call "peace," which is totally unrelated to the harmonious functioning of this body.

When you free yourself from the burden of reaching out there to grasp, to experience, and to be in that reality, then you find that it is more difficult to understand the reality of anything. You have no way of experiencing the reality of anything, you see. So at least you are not living in a

21

world of illusions; you accept that there is nothing, nothing that you can do to experience the reality of anything, except the reality that is imposed on us by the society. We have to accept the reality as it is imposed on us by the society because it is very essential for us to function in this world intelligently and sanely. If we don't accept that reality, we are lost—we end up in the loony bin. We have to accept the reality as it is imposed on us by culture, by society or whatever you want to call it, and at the same time understand there is nothing that you can do to experience the reality of anything. Then you cannot be in conflict with the society, and also the demand to be something other than what you are also comes to an end.

The goal that you have placed before yourself—rather the goal, which you have accepted as the ideal goal to be reached—is not there. The demand to be something other than what you are also is not there. It is not a question of accepting it, but the pursuit of those goals, which the culture has placed before us, and we have accepted as the desirable ones, is not there any more, so the demand to reach that goal also is not there any more. So, you are what you are. The movement in the direction of becoming something other than what you are, isn't there any more. So you are not in conflict with yourself. If you are not in conflict with yourself, you cannot be in conflict with the society around you.

You are not at peace with yourself, so it is not possible for you to be at peace with others. Even then there is no guarantee that your neighbors will be peaceful. You are not concerned with that, you see. You are at peace with yourself, and the consequences of that are really difficult to face. Then you become a threat to the society as it functions today. You become a threat to your neighbors also because they have accepted the reality of the world as real, and they are pursuing some funny thing called "peace", and so you will become a threat to their existence as they know it and as they experience it. So you are all alone—not the aloneness that people want to avoid—you are all alone.

It's not the ultimate reality that one is interested in, or the techniques and systems and methods that he is using to achieve whatever the goal is, but the running of the motor there. Not the teachings of the gurus, not the teachings of the holy men, not the techniques (umpteen number of them you have), which will give you the energy that you are seeking. But that one, if that movement is not there, is the thing that will set in motion and release the energy that is there. It doesn't have to be the holy man's teaching. It doesn't have to be any techniques that man has invented. Because there is no friction there—you really don't know what it is.

The movement there and the movement here is one—there is energy there. So that you say is a mechanical energy, but this is also a mechanical energy, this is also a machine. The human machine is no different from the machine out there—both of them are in unison. Whatever energy is there, the same energy is in operation here. So, any other energy you experience through the practice of any techniques is a frictional energy—that energy is created by the friction of thought. The demand to experience that energy is the one that is responsible for the energy you experience. But *this* energy is something that cannot be experienced at all. This is just an expression of life, a manifestation of life.

You don't have to do a thing. Anything you do to experience that is preventing the possibility of that energy that is already there, which is the expression of life, which is the manifestation of life, to function there. But it has no value in terms of the values we give to whatever we are doing—the techniques, meditation, yoga, and all that. I am not against any one of those things. Please don't get me wrong. But they are not the means to achieve the goal that you have placed before yourself—the goal itself is false. If the suppleness of the body is the goal you have before you, probably the techniques of yoga will help you to keep the body supple. But that is not the instrument to reach the goal of enlightenment or transformation or whatever you want to call it—or, even the techniques of meditation—all those are self-centered activities. They are all self-perpetuating mechanisms, which you use. So the object of your search for the ultimate reality is defeated by all these techniques because these techniques are self-perpetuating instruments. Then you will suddenly realize, or it dawns on you, that the very search for the ultimate reality is also a self-perpetuating mechanism. There is nothing to reach, nothing to gain, nothing to attain.

As long as you are doing something to attain whatever your goal is, so long this is a self-perpetuating mechanism. When I use the word "self-perpetuating" mechanism—I don't mean that there is a self or an entity, but it has this self-perpetuating mechanism. I have to use the word "self" because there is no other word. You know, the self-starter you have in the car—the self-igniting things. Like that, it perpetuates itself. That is all that it is interested in.

Anything you want to achieve is a self-centered activity. When I use the term "self-centered activity," you always translate it in terms of something that should be avoided—because selflessness is the goal before you. As long as you are doing something to be selfless, so long you are a self-centered individual. When this movement in the direction of wanting to be a selfless man is not there, then there is no self; there is no self-centered activity. It is the very techniques, the systems and methods that you are using to reach your goal of selflessness, which are self-centered activity.

When once that demand is not there anymore ... unfortunately, the society (or culture or whatever you want to call it) has placed before us the perfect goal, the ideal goal, which is the goal of everybody. Because a selfless man will be a great asset to the society, and the society is interested only in continuity—the status quo. So all those values, which we have accepted as the values that one should cultivate, are invented by the human mind to keep itself going.

The goal is the one that is making it possible for you to continue this way, but you are not getting anywhere. The hope is that one day, through some miracle or through the help of somebody, you will be able to reach the goal. It is the hope that keeps you going, but actually and factually you are not getting anywhere. You will realize somewhere along the line that whatever you are doing to reach your goal is not leading you anywhere. Then you want to try this, that and the other. But if you try one and that doesn't work, you will see that all the other systems are exactly the same. This has to be very, very clear, you see. Whatever pursuit you are indulging in, if I may use that word, somewhere along the line it has to dawn on you that it is not leading you anywhere.

As long as you want something, so long you will do that. That want has to be very, very clear. What do you want? That is why all the time I ask you the question, "What do you want?" You say, "I want to be at peace with myself." That is an impossible goal for you because everything you are doing to be at peace with yourself is the one that is destroying the peace that is already there. You have set in motion the movement of thought, which is destroying the peace that is there. I don't know if it is clear to you, anyway, it is very difficult to understand that all that you are doing is the impediment, is the one that is disturbing the harmony, the peace that is already there.

Any movement, in any direction, on any level, is a very destructive factor for the smooth functioning and the peaceful functioning of this living organism, which is not at all interested in your spiritual experiences. It has no interest in any one of those spiritual experiences, however extraordinary they may be. When once you have one spiritual experience there is bound to be a demand for more and more of the same, and ultimately you will want to be in that state permanently. There is no such thing as permanent happiness, permanent bliss, at all. I can say that—probably you think that there is, because all those books talk of eternal bliss, permanent bliss, and permanent happiness. And you know jolly well that it is not leading you anywhere. The mechanism that is involved, the instrument that you are using, is the one that keeps you going because it does not know anything else. It has come into being through so many years of hard work, effort and will—that itself is effort, that itself is will. Your wanting to be in a state of effortlessness through the use of effort is not going to succeed. So forget about the effortless state—it doesn't exist at all. If you want to be in an effortless state through effort—how the hell are you going to achieve that goal? You forget that everything you are doing, any movement that is there, any want that is there, for whatever reason you want to be in an effortless state, is effort.

You cannot achieve that goal of effortlessness. Effortlessness is something which cannot be achieved through effort. So is there anything that you can do to stop the effort? Even that also is an effort. It is really a maddening thing. Thank God you have not pushed yourself, really, into that corner. Then you see, you will really go crazy. You are frightened of that. That is impossible! You have to see that everything you are doing to be in that effortless state, for whatever reason you want to be in there, is effort. Even wanting not to use effort also is effort. The total absence of will and the total absence of effort, of all and every kind, may be called an effortless state; but that effortless state is not something that you can achieve through effort—not at all possible.

I don't know if you have ever understood the meaninglessness of what you are doing. You can change the techniques, you can change the teachers, but basically and essentially, the very teaching that you are using to reach your goal is the obstacle. It doesn't matter what teacher you follow. If you question the teaching, unfortunately, you have to question the teacher himself. So then comes the sentiment: "Something is wrong with me, one day I am going to understand." If it is not possible for you to understand today, you are not going to understand at all. So the understanding is the absence of the demand for understanding—either now or tomorrow.

Now, there is no understanding necessary. The understanding is only for the purpose of understanding something tomorrow—not today. Today you don't have to understand a thing at all.

It may sound funny to you, but that's the way it is. So what do you want to understand? You can't understand me at all. I have been talking for 20 days and I can go on, but you are not going to understand anything at all. It's not that it is difficult. It is so simple. The complex structure that is involved is the very thing that does not accept the simplicity of it. That is really the problem—it can't be that simple—because that structure is so complex that it doesn't want even to consider the possibility that it could be so simple. So you are going to understand tomorrow, not today. Tomorrow it is the same story, and then after 10 years it is the same story. So what do you do about this situation? We all have been through that—and actually and literally went mad. Either you flip or fly—the chances of flipping are really good if you push yourself into a corner. You are not going to do that.

What do you want to understand? I am not saying anything profound. I have been repeating the same thing day after day, day after day. It's not something that the thought is manufacturing here. It's not a thought-manufactured or logically ascertained premise that I am putting across to you. Basically, it sounds very contradictory to you. What I am actually doing—you don't understand what I am doing—is that I make a statement and the second statement is negating the first statement. Sometimes you see some contradictions in what I am saying. Actually they are not contradictions.

So, this statement does not express what I am trying to express, so the second statement is negating the first statement, the third statement is negating the first two statements, and the fourth statement is negating the previous three statements. Not with the idea of arriving at any goal. Not with the idea of communicating anything to you. There is nothing to be communicated—only this series of negations. Not with the idea of arriving at any goal. The goal is understanding—so you want to understand, you see. There is nothing to understand here. Every time you make some sense out of it, I am trying to point out that's not it.

It is not the doctrine of *neti-neti*. In India they have evolved this negative approach. But the so-called negative approach is a positive approach, because still they are interested in reaching the goal. They have failed through the positive approaches, so they have invented what is called the negative approach—"Not this, not this, not this." The unknown cannot be reached or experienced through the positive approach. So they have failed. So then, you see the so-called negative approach is not really a negative approach because the goal is still a positive goal of knowing the unknown, for example, or wanting to experience something which cannot be experienced. So, this movement, which has adopted a negative approach, is still interested in the positive goal of knowing the unknown, experiencing something which cannot be experienced.

It's only a trick. That's all it is—playing with itself. As long as the goal is a positive goal, no matter what the goal is, so long any approach, whether it is called positive or negative, is not a negative approach, it is a positive approach. It's all right to play games with you, it's interesting, but there is no

28

such thing as the "beyond," no such thing as the "unknown." If you accept that there is such a thing as the unknown, you will do something or the other to know the unknown. Your interest is to know. So this movement is not going to stop as long as it is interested in experiencing something that cannot be experienced.

That means that there is still something that cannot be experienced. There is no such thing as the unknown at all. So, how can you say that there is no such thing as the unknown? How can you make such a dogmatic assertion? You will find out. As long as you are pursuing the unknown, so long this movement is in operation. There is something that you can do—you see that gives you the hope—maybe one day you will stumble into this to experience the unknown. How can the unknown, if there is any unknown, ever become part of the known? Not a chance. Even assuming for a moment that this movement (which is demanding to know the unknown) is not there, what is there you will never know. You have no way of knowing that at all, no way of capturing that and experiencing that or giving expression to it.

So to talk of that bliss, the eternal bliss, love, and all that, is romantic poetry, because you have no way of capturing that and containing it and giving expression to it. This dawns on you that this is not the movement, this is not the instrument that can help you to understand anything, and there is no other instrument. So then there is nothing to understand.

I don't want to talk, to give a talk—you help me.

You see, if you translate what I am saying in terms of your values, in terms of ethical codes of conduct, you are really missing the point. It is not that I am against the moral codes of conduct. They have a social value, for the smooth functioning of the society they are essential. You will have to have some code of conduct for functioning in this world intelligently; otherwise there will be utter chaos in this world. That is essential, that's a social problem; it is not an ethical problem, it's not a religious problem at all.

You have to separate the two things, because we are living in a different world today. Not because they are bad, but because they are unsuitable to the present occasion, so we have to find some other way of keeping ourselves in harmony with the world around us. But as long as you are in conflict within yourself, so long it will not be possible for you to be in harmony with the society around you. You are yourself responsible for that.

I am afraid if you translate the statements that I am making within the framework of your religious thinking, you are really missing the point. It has nothing to do with it at all. I am not suggesting that you should change yourself into something other than what you are—it is just not possible. I am not trying to free you from anything. I don't think there is any purpose in this talking, but in the light of the description, maybe you will realize that the image you have of whatever you are after has no relationship whatsoever. So you can brush aside my description and say it is nonsense, that's your privilege, but maybe it will occur to you that the image you have of your goal or the image of what you are going to be one day, through all the effort and will which you are using, has absolutely no relationship whatsoever with what I am describing.

This is not really what you are interested in. I was telling you the other day, "I wish I could give you just a glimpse of it." Not glimpse in the sense in which you use the word "glimpse"—a touch of it. You wouldn't want to touch this at all. And what you want, what you are interested in, doesn't exist.

You can have a lot of petty experiences if that is what you are interested in—do all the meditations, do everything you want, you see you will have lots of them. It's a lot easier to experience those things by taking drugs. I am not recommending drugs, but they are the same, exactly the same.

The doctors say that drugs will damage the brain, but this will also damage the brain if it is done very seriously, some of those things. That's why they have gone crazy, jumped into the river and killed themselves. They did all kinds of things—locked themselves up in caves—because they couldn't face it.

You see, it is not possible for you to watch your thoughts; it is not possible for you to watch every step you take. It will drive you crazy. You can't walk. That's not what is meant by this idea that you should be aware of everything and watch your thoughts—how is it possible for you to watch every thought of yours? And for what do you want to watch your thoughts? What for? Control? It's not possible for you to control.

It is a tremendous momentum, you see. When you succeed in your imagination that you have controlled your thoughts and experienced some space between two thoughts or some thoughtless state, or whatever you want to call it, you feel that you are getting somewhere. That is a thought-induced state of thoughtlessness. That's a thought-induced space between two thoughts. The fact that you experience those states—space between two thoughts and the thought-less state—means that the thought was very, very much there. It surfaces afterwards like the River Rhone, which flows through France—somewhere it disappears and then it comes up again; it has gone underground. That does not mean that the river is not there; it is still there. You can't use it for purposes of navigation, but ultimately it comes up again. In exactly the same way, all these things you are pushing down into the subterranean regions, and you feel that you are experiencing something extraordinary, but it surfaces again and then you find that those thoughts are welling up inside of you.

You are not aware that you are breathing now. You don't have to be conscious of your breathing. Why do you want to be conscious of your breathing and control your breathing? To expand your lungs, do what you like with your chest—that's a different matter. But why do you want to be aware of the movement of breath from the origin to the end—whatever is the end? Then you suddenly become conscious of your breathing. Your breath and thought are very closely related. That's why you want to control your breath. And that, in a way, is controlling the thought for a while. But if you hold your breath for long, it is going to choke you to death in exactly the same way that anything you do to hold or block the flow of thought is going to choke you to death, literally to death, or it will damage something there—it's a very powerful vibration. Thought is after all a vibration. What is thought? An extraordinary vibration; it is like an atom.

You can't play with those things at all—except the petty experiences you have when you manipulate those things. For what purpose? You are not going to reach your goal of completely controlling your thought. It has to function in its own way, in its disconnected, disjointed way. That is something that cannot be brought about through any effort of yours. It has to fall into its normal rhythm. Even if you want to make it fall into the normal rhythm, you are adding momentum to that. That has a life of its own; it has, unfortunately, established a parallel life within the movement of life. These two are always in conflict. You see, as I was saying yesterday, thought has become the master of this body. It's not that it has totally mastered the whole thing, but it is still trying to control everything that is there. You cannot pull the servant out of the household, no matter what you do. If you forcibly do it, he will burn the whole household, and then only knowing very well that he will also be burned. It's a foolish thing for him, but that's what he is going to do if he tries. Don't push these similes to the logical conclusions, but you will find out for yourself when you do these things, not just take them lightly—take them lightly and play with them, it's all right—toys.

Q: *Just float along? Nothing to pursue, just float?*

U.G.: Even that "floating" is not a voluntary thing on your part. You don't have to do a thing. You are not separate from that. That's all that I am emphasizing. You cannot separate yourself from the thought and say, "These are my thoughts." That is the illusion you have, and so you cannot be without any illusion. You always replace one illusion with another illusion. Always.

Q: *And I accept that as well.*

U.G.: You accept that you are always replacing one illusion with another illusion; so your wanting to be free from illusion is an impossibility—that itself is an illusion. Why do you want to be free from illusions? That's the end of you. It's not that I am frightening you, I am just pointing out that it is not just a lighthearted game to play. That is you, you as you know yourself—that knowledge you have of yourself is not there any more—it can't be anymore there. So when it is not there, the knowledge you have about the world also is not there any more—it can't be there any more. It is not going to come to an end that easily. It will always be replaced by another illusion.

You don't want to be a normal person; you don't want to be an ordinary person. That is really the problem. It is the most difficult thing to be an ordinary person. Culture demands that you must be something other than what you are. That has set in momentum this tremendous, powerful movement of thought, which demands that you should be something other than what you are. That's all that is there. You use it to achieve something; otherwise it has no use.

33

The only use you have for thought is to feed this body. Without thought you cannot, you won't. So that is why thought is there—and to reproduce one like this. That's all the use you have for the thought. It has no other use at all. It cannot be used to speculate.

You can build a tremendous philosophical structure of thought, but it has no value at all. You can interpret it, any event in your life, the events around you, and build up another philosophical structure of thought, but it is not intended for that.

At the same time, you forget (don't forget, rather) that everything you have around you is the creation of thought. You are yourself born out of that thought—otherwise you would not be here at all. In that sense it has a tremendous value, but yet that is the very thing that will destroy you.

That's the paradox. Everything that you have created in this world has become possible through the help of that thought, but unfortunately that very thing has become the enemy of man, because you are using that for purposes for which it is not interested—in solving the living problems. It can be used for solving the technical problems very well and efficiently, but that is something that cannot be used to solve the problems of life.

Positive thinking, positive living, very interesting, you know. You can't be always positive. How can you be positive? Anything that does not suggest your positive thinking, you call it negative. But positive and negative is only in the field of your thinking. When the thought is not there, it is neither positive nor negative. As I was saying, there is no such thing as a negative approach at all. It's a gimmick to play with.

I am telling you to stand on your own feet—you can walk, you can swim, you are not going to sink. That's all that I can say. As long as there is fear, so long the danger of your sinking there is almost certain. Otherwise, there is a buoyancy there in the water that keeps you afloat. The fear of sinking is the very thing that makes it impossible for you to let the movement happen in its own way. You see, it has no direction; it is just a movement. It has no direction. You are all the time trying to manipulate and channel that along a particular direction so that you can have some benefits out of it. You are just a movement without a direction.

Q: *Actually we are rather fond of thinking as a man, as a human being. I am wondering why is this rather funny animal thinking all the time and just building all those thoughts?*

U.G.: I will ask you the question. You tell me, when do you think? Not why do you think—that's not the question. When do you think? I am asking you a question, when do you think?

Q: *As far as I know, all the time.*

U.G.: All the time, and for what? What is responsible for your thinking? You haven't yet answered my question—when do you think? When you want something, you think. It is very clear to me.

Q: *Not at all.*

U.G.: Of course. You don't even know that you are thinking. Do you know that you are thinking now? It's an automatic thing.

Q: *It's an automatic thing, that's right.*

U.G.: It's automatic. You don't even know that you are thinking—and so why this sudden interest in wanting to find out why you are thinking? I don't even know that I am talking. You don't even know that you are talking. When you asked your question, "Am I thinking?" you would say, "Yes." That "yes" also is an automatic thing.

Q: *I don't care if it's automatic or not.*

U.G.: The whole thing is on automatic. Whatever is put in there, when you are stimulated, it comes out. To use the jargon of the computer language—the input has to be there. So, this has been going on and on and on and on. When there is stimulation, it comes out. If it is not there, you see, it stops. So that's the reason why you go on, acquiring this knowledge, feeding it all the time—it's in the computer.

So, after all, it's an automatic thing that is there. What do you know? You know a lot. You have gathered all this from various sources and filled it up. Most of it is not necessary. You know a lot and you want to know more and more and more—to use it, of course. There's no such thing as knowledge for the sake of knowledge. It gives me power, it gives you power. Knowledge is power. "I know; you don't know." So that gives you power. You may not even be conscious of that. Your knowing more than the other gives you power. In that sense, knowledge is power. To acquire more and more knowledge, other than the knowledge that is essential for the survival of the living organism, is to acquire more and more power over others.

Except for the technical knowledge that you need to make a living—that is understandable—that's all. I have to learn a technique; otherwise the society is not going to feed me unless I give something in return. And what they want, they know. You have to give them what they want, not what you have to give. What have you to give? You have nothing to give anyway. Otherwise what value has this knowledge for you—to know more about something, which you really do not know?

We are all the time talking about thought and thinking. I am asking you the question, "What is thought?" Have you ever looked at thought—let along controlling thought; let alone manipulating thought; let alone using that thought for achieving something material or otherwise? You cannot look at your thought, because you cannot separate yourself from thought and look at it. The knowledge you have about thought is all that is there. There is no thought independent or apart from the knowledge you have about those thoughts—the definitions you have. So if somebody asks you the question, "What is thought?", any answer you have is the answer that is put in there—the answers that others have given, and you have, by combinations and permutations of those ideations and mentations about thoughts, created your own thoughts, which you call your own.

Just like mixing up different colors, you create thousands of pastel colors, but basically all of them can be reduced to only seven colors that you find in nature. What you think is yours is the combination and permutation of all those thoughts, just the way you have created hundreds and hundreds of pastel colors. You have created your own ideas. That is what you call "thinking." So when you want to look at thought, what is there is only all of what you know about thought—otherwise you can't look at thought. There is no thought other than what is there, what you know about thought. That's all that I am saying. So when that is understood, the meaninglessness of the whole business of wanting to look at thought comes to an end. Because it is not possible, what is there is only what you know, the definitions given by others, and out of those definitions, if you are very intelligent and clever enough, you create your own definitions. That's all.

So it is like any other object you have around you—there are so many objects. When you look at it, the knowledge you have about that comes into your head. There is an illusion that the thought is something different. So it is you that creates the object. The object may be there, but the knowledge you have about that object is all that you know. Apart from that knowledge and independent of that knowledge, free from that knowledge, you have no way of knowing anything about it. You have no way of directly experiencing anything. When I use the word "directly" it does not mean that there is any other way of experiencing things. That's the wrong word, "directly"—it implies that there is some other way of experiencing things, directly, other than the way that you are experiencing things. The knowledge you have about it is all that is there and that is what you are experiencing. Really, you don't know what it is.

In exactly the same way, when you want to know something about thought, experience thought, it is the same process that is in operation there. There is no inside and outside. What is there is only the operation, the flow of the knowledge. So you cannot actually separate yourself from thought and look at it.

So when once such a question is thrown at you, what should happen is that giving all the answers has no meaning because all that is acquired and taught. So that movement stops. There is no need for you to answer the question. There is no need for you to know anything about it. All that you know comes to a halt—not literally—it has no momentum any more, it slows down. So, then it dawns upon you the meaninglessness of trying to answer that question, because it has really no answer at all. The answers that others have given are there. So you have nothing to say on that thing called thought, because all you can say is what you have gathered from other sources, and so you have no answer of your own.

Q: *Even then we can have a little conversation.*

U.G.: All right. All right.

Q: *Apart from the question of if it is meaningful or meaningless...*

U.G.: All right, yes.

Q: *There still are things, like walls and people around you. And what we know about it, what we see about it...*

U.G.: But that is not what that person is. You don't know actually anything about that person or that thing, except what you are projecting on that object or the individual, the knowledge you have about it, and this knowledge is the experience. It goes on and on. That's all. What that really is, you have no way of knowing.

Q: *That is what I do understand. And when we are speaking about reality, we can speak about our knowledge about it and call this knowledge "reality."*

U.G.: What for? Then it becomes a classroom discussion or a discussion in a debating society, each one trying to show that he knows more, a lot more, than the other. What do you get out of it? Each one is trying to prove that he knows more than you do, to win you over to his point of view.

Q: *What I am trying to ask is, is there any chance—I understand that there is no method—but is there any chance of getting out of this knowledge of reality, to reality?*

U.G.: If you are lucky enough (it's only luck) to get out of this trap of the knowledge, the question of reality is not there any more. Because the question is thrown out by this knowledge, which is still interested in finding out the reality of things, and to experience for yourself directly what the reality is all about. When this is not there, the question is also not there. So there is no need for finding out any answer. Because this question, which you are posing to yourself and also putting it to me, is born out of the assumption that there is a reality, and that assumption is born out of this knowledge you have of and about the reality. So when this is not there, the knowledge is not there, the knowledge is the answer you already have—it is why you are asking the question—the question automatically goes.

What is necessary is not to find out the answer to the question, but understand that the question which you are asking, posing to yourself, and putting it to somebody, is born out of the answer you already have, which is the knowledge. So, the question and answer format, if we indulge in it for long, becomes a meaningless ritual—the question and answer business. If you are really interested in finding out the reality, this has to dawn on you, that your very questioning mechanism is born out of the answers that you already have. Otherwise there can't be any question—because there is an assumption on your part that there is a reality, first of all, and then, that there is something that you can do to experience the reality of things without the knowledge. The knowledge gives you the experience of reality. That is for sure. So, if this is not there, is there any other way of experiencing the reality? You are asking the question. The question goes with the answer. So there is no need to ask questions and there is no need to answer.

I am not trying to be clever. I am just spotlighting what is involved in the question and answer business. I am not actually answering any of your questions. I am just pointing out that you cannot have any questions when what you have is the answers.

Q: *I do understand, and even then I would like to continue the game.*

U.G.: Fine. Maybe you are good at the game. I am not. Anyway we will see what we can do.

Q: *Even though you know our preoccupation with knowledge about it, about anything, you are talking about reality to us and about accepting reality.*

U.G.: As it is.

Q: *As it is?*

U.G.: As it is imposed on us by our culture for purposes of intelligent and sane functioning in this world, and yet, realizing that it has no other value other than the functional value. Otherwise we will be in trouble, you see. If you don't call this a microphone, and you decide to call it a monkey, we will all have to relearn, and every time we look at it we will have to call it a red or black monkey instead of a microphone. That's all. It is very simple, for purposes of communication.

Q: *I wonder what would happen if we did call that chair a lamp and this table a hat, because a lot of our philosophies and ideas are also linked with it.*

U.G.: The whole discussion is about that, that's all, for hours and hours. It is interesting to build a philosophical structure. That's why we have so many philosophers and so many philosophies in this world.

Q: *As far as I did understand, until now, there is only one thing worth striving for — acceptance.*

U.G.: Don't you see the contradiction in those terms? If you accept, where is the need for striving? That comes to an end. If you accept something, you cannot talk of striving at all. You accept it, you believe. You believe in something, you accept it as an act of faith, and that's the end of it. If you question that, that means you have not accepted it. You are not sure of it.

Q: *I had to accept my job as a legal officer before I could strive to acquire the knowledge...*

U.G.: ... to acquire the knowledge that is necessary to get the job. So you see, you had to struggle, and put in a lot of effort to acquire the necessary legal knowledge to get this job. That's understood. So, that is the only way. There is no other way. And, you are applying that technique to achieve your so-called spiritual goals. This is the difference that I am pointing out.

Even as a legal officer, you know that as a lawyer, I suppose—what do they do in the courts? You have always to rely upon the precedents, the previous judgments. Both lawyers quote the previous judgments and argue it out, and the judge either accepts yours or the other fellow's argument, or gives the decision either in favor of your client or the other client. Then there is a higher court; you go to the higher court. There it is the same. And you go to the Supreme Court where the judge finally decides, "This is it." So, you can disagree with the judgment, the client can do everything possible to reject it, and refuse to accept it, but he has a way of enforcing that judgment through force. If it is a civil case being sued, you will lose what you are claiming. If it is a criminal matter, you will end up in prison. Ultimately that is the man who decides who is telling a lie and who is telling the truth. It is arbitrary in the final analysis.

So it is very essential for you to be conversant with the whole structure of law. I don't want to get into it, I am not a lawyer, anyway, I am just pointing out that it is very essential for you to know the legal side of it, and acquire the legal knowledge for your job. The more efficient you are the better are your chances. The cleverer you are the better are your prospects. That is understood. So, you have to put in struggle and use effort, use your will and then you arrive, but there is always more and more to achieve. But you are using that same instrument to achieve your spiritual goals. This is all that I am pointing out.

That cannot conceive of the possibility of under-standing anything except in time. It takes time. It has taken so many years for you to be where you are today, and you are still striving and struggling to reach a higher plateau—higher and higher and higher—there are hierar-chies there. That instrument which you are using cannot conceive of the possibility of understanding anything with-out effort, without striving, without producing will. It can-not conceive of that possibility. But the issues that you have to deal with in life are the living issues. That is where this has not helped us to solve the problems. Temporarily you can find some solution, but that creates another problem, and another problem, and it goes on and on and on and on. So that is something that cannot be used to tackle the life issues. These are all life issues—the living problems. The instrument, which is not dead—the instrument we are using in other areas is a dead instrument and that cannot be used to understand anything living. That's all that I am saying.

You cannot but think in terms of striving, effort, time—one day you are going to reach the spiritual goal—just the way you have succeeded, are still trying to succeed, in the goal which you have placed before yourself.

Q: *But are you trying to say that there is some knowledge which solves the real problems of life?*

U.G.: No, not at all. That cannot help you to understand or solve the living problems. Because there are no problems there at all in that sense. We have only the solutions. You are interested only in solutions, and those solutions have not solved your problems, so you are trying to find different kinds of solutions. But the situation will remain exactly the same, yet there is somehow the hope that maybe you will find *the* solution for solving your problems.

So your problem is not the problem but the solution. If the solution is gone, there is no problem there. So you are not ready to accept that that is not the solution. If there is a solution, the problem shouldn't be there anymore. This is what I am emphasizing: if the answers are given by others, the wise men, then the questions shouldn't be there at all. So they are obviously not the answers. If they were the answers, the questions would not be there.

So why don't you question the answers? If you question the answers, you question those who have given the answers. So you take it for granted that they are all wise men; they are all spiritually superior to us all; that they know what they are talking about. They don't know a damn thing!

Why are you asking these questions, if I may ask you that counter-question? Why are you asking these questions? Where do these questions come from, first of all? Where do they originate in you? I want to hammer this point, to make you see very clearly the absurdity of asking these questions. It is very essential to ask questions to learn the technical know-how of certain things. There somebody is there to help you. If something is wrong with the television, there is always somebody who can help you out with the technical know-how, and how to set it right. That is understood. I am not talking about that at all. But

44

the questions which you are asking are of a different kind.

Where do you think these questions take their birth? How do they formulate themselves in you? They are all mechanical questions. What I am trying to emphasize all the time is that it is essential for you to understand how mechanical the whole thing is.

There is nobody who is asking the questions there. There is no questioner who is asking the questions there. There is an illusion that there is a questioner who is formulating these questions and throwing these questions at somebody and expecting somebody to answer your questions.

The answers that you get really are not the answers, because the questions persist there, in spite of the answers you think that the other chap is giving you—but the question is still there. This answer, which you think is the answer (satisfactory or otherwise), is really not the answer. If it were so, the question should go once and for all, because all the questions are variations of the same question. What I am trying to say is that you already have the answer there, and all these questions are the questions that are not interested in getting any answers. The answer, if there is any to that question, should destroy the answer you already have. So there is no questioner there. If the answer goes, along with the question, the questioner—non-existant questioner there—also has to go. I don't know if I make myself clear.

Do you have any question which you can call your own? If you can come out with a question which you can call your own, a question that has never, never been asked before, then there is a meaning in talking things over. Then you don't have to sit and ask anybody those questions, because such questions don't exist at all—a question which you can call your own, a question that has never been asked before. All the answers are there for those questions. So probably you don't realize that the questions, which you are asking, are born out of the answers you already have. So they are not your answers at all. The answers have been put in there.

Why are you asking these questions, why are you not satisfied with the answers that are already there? That is my question. Why? If you are satisfied, yes, it's all right, you say, "I don't want any answers." But still, the question is there inside of you. Whether you go and ask somebody or expect an answer from some wise man, it is still there. Why is it there?

What happens if the question comes to an end? You come to an end. You are nothing but the answers. That's all that I am saying. How can you understand? There is no questioner who is asking the questions, but the answer that is there is in great jeopardy. That is why it does not want any answer. The answer is the end of that answer you have, which is not yours, so what the hell if it is gone? Anyway, the answers you have are already dead; the answers have been given by dead persons. Anybody who repeats those answers is a dead person. A living person cannot give any answer to those questions, because any answer that you get from anybody is a dead answer, because the question is a dead question. That's the reason why I am not giving any answer to you at all.

You are living in a world of dead ideas—all the thoughts are dead, they are not living. You cannot invest them with life. That's what you are trying to do all the time; you invest them with emotions, but they are not living things. That can never touch anything living. The problems you think you have are the living problems. So, the solutions that you have are not adequate enough to handle the living problems. They are good enough to discuss in a classroom or in some sort of a ritual—a question-and-answer ritual—repeating the same old dead ideas, but those things can never, never touch anything living there, because the living thing will burn out the whole thing completely and totally.

So, you are not going to touch anything living at any time; you are not looking at anything; you are not in contact with anything living, as long as you use your thoughts to understand and experience anything. When that is not there, there is no need for you to understand and experience anything. So anything you experience only gathers momentum—adds to that—that's all. There is nothing that you can call your own.

I have no questions of *any* kind. How come you have so many questions? I am not giving any answers. So this I repeat day after day, day after day. It's the same point, hammer it out, and whether you understand it or not, is of no importance to me.

* * * * * *

What exactly do people mean when they talk of consciousness? There is no such thing as unconsciousness. You see a person unconscious and the medical technology can find out the reason why a particular individual is unconscious. So, the individual who is unconscious has no way of knowing that he is unconscious. When he comes out of that unconscious state, he becomes conscious. So do you think you are conscious now? Do you think you are awake? Do you think you are alive?

It is your thinking that makes you feel that you are alive, that you are conscious. That is possible only when the knowledge you have about things is in operation there. You have no way of finding out whether you are alive or dead. In that sense, there is no death at all, because you are not alive. You become conscious of things only when the knowledge is in operation. When the knowledge is absent, whether the person is dead or alive is of no importance to this movement of thought, which comes to an end before what we call "death" takes place.

So, it really doesn't matter whether one is alive or dead. Of course, it does matter to one who considers that it is very important, and to those who are involved with that individual, but you have no way of finding out whether you are alive or dead, or whether you are conscious or not. You become conscious only through the help of thought. But unfortunately it is there all the time. So, the suggestion that it is not possible to experience anything makes no sense to you at all, because you have no reference point there when this movement is absent. When this movement is absent, all those questions about consciousness are not there. That is what I mean by saying that the questions are absent.

How can you bring about a change in consciousness, which has no limits, which has no boundaries, which has no frontiers? They can try and spend millions and millions and millions of dollars and do every kind of research to find the seat of human consciousness, but there is no such thing as the seat of human consciousness at all. They can try—and they are going to spend billions of dollars to find out—but the chances of their succeeding in that are well nigh impossible. There is no such thing as a *seat* located in any particular individual. What is there is the thought.

Whenever the thought takes its birth there, you have created an entity or a point, and in reference to that point you are experiencing things. So, when the thought is not there, is it possible for you to experience anything or relate anything to a non-existing thing here?

Every time the thought is born, you are born. The thought in its very nature is short-lived; and once it is gone, that's the end of it. That is probably what people meant when they used this "birth and death and death and birth"—it is not that this particular entity, which is non-existing even while you are living, takes a series of births. The ending of births and deaths is the state that they are talking about. But that state cannot be described in terms of bliss, beatitude, love, compassion and all that kind of thing. That becomes poetic nonsense and romantic stuff—if you use those words, because you have no way of experiencing what is there in between these two thoughts.

The world you experience around you is also from that point of view. There must be a point and it is this point that creates the space. If this point is not there, there is no space. So, anything you experience from this point is an illusion—not that the world is an illusion. All these Vedantins and philosophers in India, particularly the students of Shankara, indulge in such frivolous, absolute nonsense. The world is not an illusion, but anything you experience in relationship with this point, which itself is illusory, is bound to be an illusion, that's all—but not that the world is an illusion. When they used the word *"maya"*, they did not mean illusion in the sense in which the English word is used. *Maya* means to measure—the Sanskrit word means to measure. You cannot measure anything unless you have a point. So, if the center is absent, there is no circumference at all. That is pure and simple basic arithmetic.

This point has no continuity. This point comes into being in response to the demands of the situation. The demands of the situation create this point. The subject does not at all exist there. It is the object that creates the subject. This runs counter to the whole philosophical thinking of man in India. The subject comes and goes and comes and goes in response to the things that are happening there. It is the object that creates the subject and not the subject that creates the object. This is a simple physiological phenomenon, which can be tested. There is an object there, for example, there is no subject here; so what creates the subject, is the object.

There is light. If the light is not there you have no way of looking at anything. The light falls on that object and the reflection of that light activates the optic nerve, which in turn activates the memory cells. When once the memory

49

cells are activated, all the knowledge you have about it comes into operation. It is that thing that is happening there that has created the subject, which is the knowledge you have about that. The word "microphone" is the I. There is nothing there other than the word microphone. When you reduce it to that, you feel the absurdity of talking about the self—the lower self, the higher self and knowing self, self-knowing, self-knowledge, knowing from moment-to-moment is absolute rubbish, balderdash! You can indulge in such absolute nonsense and build up philosophical theories, but there is no subject there at all at any time. It is not the subject that creates the object.

Not only the "I" but all the physical sensations are involved in this. The sound, the olfactory nerves, the smell, and the sense of touch, any one of these sensations in operation, necessarily have to bring the subject. There is not one continuous subject who is gathering all these experiences and piling them up together, adding them up together, and says "This is me," but everything is discontinuous, a disconnected one—the sound is one, the physical seeing is one, the smelling is one. Unfortunately man, they say, has developed 4,000 nuances, these olfactory nerves, which are worthless for the purpose of the survival of the living organism.

The sense of touch means the vibration of the sound creates the subject there. So it comes and goes, comes and goes, comes and goes. There is no permanent entity there at all. What you call "I" is only a first person singular pronoun. Nothing else. If you don't want to use that word "I" so you can prove that you are a man without "I", it is your privilege. That's all that is there. There is no permanent entity there at all.

While you are living, the knowledge that is there does not belong to you. So, why are you concerned about what will happen after what you call "you" is gone? The physical body is functioning from moment-to-moment because that is the way the sensory perceptions are. To talk of living from moment-to-moment, by creating a thought-induced state of mind, has no meaning to me, except in terms of the physical functioning of the body, that is, in any case, functioning from moment-to-moment.

When the thought is not there all the time, what is happening there is living from moment-to-moment. It's all frames, millions and millions and millions of frames are there, to put it in the language of film. There is no continuity there; there is no movement there. The thought can never, never capture the movement. It is only when you invest the thought with emotion, you try to capture the movement; but actually the thought can never capture any movement that is there around you.

The movement of life is the movement of life out there and here.

Q.: *They are together?*

U.G.: They are together always.

Thought is essential only for the survival of this living organism. When it is necessary, it is there. When it is not necessary, the question of whether it is there or not is of no importance at all. So you cannot talk of that state in poetic, romantic language.

If there *is* one, he won't be hiding somewhere. He will be there shining like the star. You can't keep such people under a bushel. To be an individual is not an easy thing, you see. That means you are very ordinary. It is very difficult to be ordinary, you know. You want to be something other than what you are. To be yourself is very easy—you don't have to do a thing. No effort is necessary. You don't have to exercise will. You don't have to do anything to be yourself. But to be something other than what you are, you have to do a lot of things.

51

Part II

I Cannot Create The Hunger In You

Q: *I don't know if what happened to me one day was the same or not the same, I don't care, but I was really afraid of dying, and also of not being able to breathe any more. As soon as I feel something coming up like that, I am scared to death.*

U.G.: Yes. That prevented the possibility of the physical body going through the process of actual physical dying. The body has to go through it, because every thought that everybody felt before you, every experience that everybody experienced before you, every feeling that everybody felt before you—all that is part of your being.

So, you can't come into your own unless the whole thing is completely and totally flushed out (if I may use that word), out of your system. That is something which you cannot do or make happen with any effort or volition of your own. So, when the time comes, you may not have asked for it—you will never ask for the end of you as you know yourself, as you experience yourself. Sometimes it does happen, you see. So the fear of something coming to an end, the fear of what you know as yourself and as you experience yourself, prevented the possibility of the whole thing snapping out there. If you were lucky enough that would have happened and the whole thing would have fallen into its natural rhythm, which is discontinuous and disconnected.

That is the way the thought functions. There is no

continuity of thought. The only way it can maintain its continuity is through the constant demand for experiencing the same thing over and over and over again. So, what is there is the knowledge you have about yourself and about the world around you. The world around you is not quite different from the world you have created for yourself inside of you.

I don't want to give a talk.

What you are frightened of—not you, but that movement of thought is frightened of the continuity coming to an end. It projects always, the fear.

Q: *When I was two years old I also dreamt that I couldn't get air. So, I think that's an excuse.*

U.G.: True, but it is not an easy thing, you know, to go through that. There is a tremendous effort on your part to prevent the whole thing from being sucked into something like a vacuum cleaner. The whole of your energy, everything that is there, is drawn into something—like sucking everything that is there into this sort of vacuum cleaner. That's a very frightening situation. So the fear is its protective mechanism.

Q: *I see.*

U.G.: The physical fear is altogether different. The physical fear is very simple. That physical fear is there only for the survival of the living organism. You have, through your thinking and experiences, built on the foundation of that physical fear (which is essential for survival), what you call "psychological fear"—the fear of what you know coming to an end.

The body knows that it is immortal. I very deliberately use the word "immortal" because nothing there comes to an end. The way it is put together, when what you call clinical death takes place, it breaks itself into its constituent elements. That's all that happens. It may not reconstitute again and create the same body, which you think is yours, but at the same time, when once it breaks itself into its constituent elements, it provides the basis for the continuity of life. So, it may not be of any consolation or great feeling of happiness to the individual who is dying, but this becomes food for the millions and millions of bacteria. So, even assuming for a moment that you resort to cremation as they do in some countries, the carbon, which is the end result of the burned body, provides the basis for something coming out of the earth—some tiny little flower coming out of the earth where you dumped the ashes. So, nothing here is lost.

When there is actually a physical danger—the danger of the extinction of your physical body, which you think is yours—then everything that it has at its resource gets thrown into that situation and tries to survive in that particular moment. I don't know if you have ever noticed that when there is a real physical danger your thinking mechanism is never there to help you? Never there! So you can plan ahead for every possible situation and be prepared to meet every kind of situation in your life, but actually when there is a physical danger, all your planning and all that you have thought about to be prepared to meet every kind of danger and every kind of situation, it is just not there. So it has to fall back on its own resources. If for some reason it cannot renew itself and survive in that particular situation, it goes merrily and gracefully. It knows that nothing is lost.

This living organism is not interested in the continuity in terms of years. This is functioning from moment-to-moment. So all these religious people who are trying to interpret the religious texts in terms of living from moment-to-moment—it is a thought-induced state of mind. The sensory perceptions function from moment-to-moment. There is no continuity of your physical seeing; there is no continuity of your physical hearing; there is no continuity of your smelling; there is no continuity when you eat something; there is no continuity in the sense of touch—they are all disconnected and disjointed.

But the thought, in its interest to maintain itself and to continue without any interruption, demands these experiences all the time. That is the only way it can maintain its continuity. The body functions in a completely different way; and it is not interested in the activity of the thought. The only thought that is necessary for this body is the thought that it has to use for the survival of the living organism.

Even if you do not feed this body, it is not concerned about it. It has certain resources, which you have built up through years of your eating. It falls back and lives on it, and when that is finished, it goes. So, for a day or two probably you feel the hunger tantrums at the same time that you regularly eat, but the body is not really concerned whether you feed the body or do not feed the body.

At the same time, it is foolish and perverse not to feed the body, hoping that you will attain some spiritual goals. That's what they do in India, they put the body through all kinds of stresses and strains—torture it—because they feel that through this endurance they will be able to achieve whatever their spiritual goals may be.

There is nothing that you can do to make that happen through any will of yours, through any effort of yours, through any volition of yours. That is the reason why I always maintain that if this kind of a thing happens it is not something mysterious—the thought falling into its natural rhythm of discontinuous and disconnected functioning—that's all, that's all that is there.

Then thought is in harmony with the sensory perceptions, the activity of the senses. So there is no conflict there; there is no struggle there; there is no pain there. There is a harmonious relationship between the two. Whenever there is a need for thought, that thought is always there to act. The act that this body is interested in is only the action that is essential for the survival of the living organism. It is not interested in any ideas you have about your religious goals or material goals. It is not at all interested. There is always this constant battle between these two things.

The thought is not something mysterious, which is what the culture has put in there, which is, of course, society—they are not different, culture and society. The society is interested in its continuity and permanence. It is interested in the status quo. It is always maintaining that status quo. That is where thought is helpful for the society and it says, "If you don't act that way, if you don't think that way, you will become anti-social, because all your actions will become thoughtless, impulsive actions." It is interested in channeling every thought of yours in that particular direction which maintains the status quo of the society. That's why there is basically, essentially and fundamentally a conflict between these two.

The culture, which is not yours, which is not mine, but we have adopted and accepted to use it as a means of survival, that's all—that has a momentum of its own, totally unrelated to the survival of the body. As long as you use that, so long you are not an individual at all. You can become an individual only when you break away from the totality of that wisdom.

There's no such thing as your mind or my mind. Maybe there is such a thing as the "world mind" where all the cumulative knowledge and the experiences are accumulating and are passed on from generation to generation. We have to use that to function in this world sanely and intelligently. If we don't use it, as I was saying the other day, we will end up on the funny farm singing loony tunes and merry melodies. So you don't want to become part of the society, you give up, and that's the end of you. And the society is still interested in fitting every individual into that framework and maintaining its continuity.

(U.G. sighs and says quietly,) I don't want to give a talk. I don't know if I have made myself clear...

That's the reason why I am all the time emphasizing the physical aspect—not with the idea of selling something, but to emphasize this and express it—what you call "enlightenment, liberation, moksha, mutation, transformation"—only in pure and simple physical and physiological (both are the same, physical and physiological) terms. To emphasize, I use those two words "physical" and "physiological," and there is *absolutely* no religious content to it and no mystical overtones or undertones to this functioning of the body. But unfortunately for centuries they have interpreted the whole thing in religious terms and that has created the misery for us all. The more you try to revive or push it through the back door, when there is no interest in the religious life of the man, you are only adding more and more to the misery, that's all.

I am not interested in propagating this. This is not something that you can make happen, nor is it possible for me to create that hunger, which is essential to understand anything. I repeat this again and again, but repetition has its own charm.

You are assuming for a moment that you are hungering for spiritual attainments and you are all the time reaching out to reach your goal. And so you see, naturally, there are so many people in the marketplace—all these saints, selling all kinds of shoddy pieces of spiritual goods. For whatever reason they are doing it, it's not our concern, but they are doing it. They say it is for the welfare of mankind and that they do it out of compassion for mankind and all that kind of thing. All that is bullshit anyway. What I am trying to say is that you are satisfied with the crumbs they throw at you. And they promise that one day they are going to deliver to you a full loaf of bread. That is just a promise. They cannot deliver the goods at all. They just don't have it. They can only cut it into pieces and distribute it to the people. When people ask me some questions, I answer in a very funny way the question about Jesus materializing loaves of bread. I said and repeat it, that he did not materialize loaves and loaves of bread, but he just got whatever bread was available there and divided it into small bits and distributed it to everybody there. Naturally, you want to attribute it to some miracle.

What I am saying is that the hunger has got to burn itself up. Every day I am saying the same thing but using different words, you see, putting these things in different ways. That's all that I can do. My vocabulary is very, very limited; so I have to use the words again and again and emphasize the same thing all over again to point out that the hunger—if there is, to find out for yourself and by yourself—it has to burn itself up.

There is no use feeding yourself with all these kinds of junk food. There is no use waiting for something to happen to satisfy your hunger. There is no point in satisfying that hunger. The hunger has to burn itself up—literally it has to burn itself out.

Even physical hunger has to burn itself out so that the physical death can take place. Just the way you feel thirsty, you know you are satisfied with these dozens of thirst-quenchers that they are advertising—Pepsi Cola, Coca-Cola, Fanta, God knows what—all of them. They are all supposed to be the thirst quenchers, but they really do not do anything there. The thirst for it has to burn itself out. Actual dehydration of the body takes place. Thank God the physical body has certain things to protect itself when the physical dehydration takes place. I don't know if you have meditated for hours and hours—the whole body reaches a point where dehydration takes place. Then you have these life-savers there in your body—the saliva—there is a profuse saliva coming out to quench your thirst and save you in that particular situation when you push this body to do certain things, through meditation, yoga, all kinds of things people do—overdo these things.

There is one thing that I am emphasizing all the time—it is not because of what you do or what you do not do that this kind of a thing happens. And why it happens to one individual and not another—there is no answer to that question. I assure you that it is not the man who has prepared himself, or purified himself for whatever reason to be ready to receive that kind of a thing. It is the other way around. It hits but it hits at random. That is the way nature operates. Lightning hits you somewhere. It is not interested in whether it is hitting a tree that is blooming or if it has fruits and is helping the people by providing shade, etc., but it just hits at random. In exactly the same way it happens to a particular individual, and that happening is acausal—it has no cause.

There are so many things happening in nature, which cannot be attributed to any particular cause. So, you are interested in studying the lives or the biographies of those people whom you think were enlightened, or god-men or some such thing, to find a clue as to how it happened to them, so that you can use whatever technique they used and make the same thing happen to you. That is your interest. Those people are giving you some techniques, some system, some methods which don't work at all. They create the hope that somehow, through some miracle, one day it is going to happen to you. But it will never happen.

I have said my piece. And I have to repeat this again and come to it from ten different angles, depending upon the nature of the questions which you throw at me, but all questions are exactly the same, as I said yesterday. Because the questions spring from the answers you already have. The answers given by others are not really the answers. I am not giving any answers to you. If I am foolish enough to give you the answers you have to understand that this very answer, which you think is the answer, is destroying the possibility of that question disappearing.

You have to take my word—I don't care if you take my word or not—that such questions never, never, never occur to me.

I have no questions of any kind except the questions I need to ask somebody, "Where can I rent a car?" "What is the quickest way to go to Brussels?" Such questions, "Which way to Rotterdam—this road or that road?" That's all. For such questions, there are always people who can help you. But those questions have no answers.

When this dawns on you that such questions have no answers, and as a matter of fact those questions spring from the answers you already have, what is necessary in that situation is the complete and total blasting of the answers that you have. That is something which you cannot make happen. It is not in your hands.

So you think the situation is hopeless; it is not hopeless. The hope is here. The hope is not there. You are waiting for something to happen tomorrow. Tomorrow *nothing* will happen! Whatever has to happen, that has got to happen *now*.

The possibility of that happening now is practically and well nigh impossible, because the instrument that you are using is the past. Unless the past comes to an end, there cannot be any present—the now, the present moment. And that present moment is something which cannot be captured by you, cannot be experienced by you. Even assuming for a moment that the past has come to an end, you have no way of knowing that it has come to an end. Then there is no future for you at all. There may be a future tomorrow —you will become the boss of your company, or the school teacher becomes the head of the institution, and the professor becomes the dean—that possibility is there, but you have to put in a lot of struggle and that takes time. You are applying the same technique—that is the only thing, that instrument which you are using, to realize whatever you are interested in, and so it puts it out there as a goal in the future. It has produced tremendous results in this world. So, how can that instrument not be the instrument to achieve your spiritual goals, if there are any spiritual goals? So that is not the instrument, obviously, because you have tried, you have done everything possible—even those who are burning with hunger to find it—it's impossible.

In India everybody has tried this—you wouldn't believe it—not one was lucky enough. Whenever such a thing has happened, it happened to those people who had given up completely and totally all their search. That is an absolute requisite for that kind of a thing. The whole movement has to slow down and come to a stop. But anything you do to make it stop is only adding momentum to it. That's really the crux of the problem.

What you are interested in doesn't exist. It's your own imagination, based upon the knowledge you have about those things. And so, there is nothing that you can do about it. You are chasing something that does not exist at all. I can say that until the cows return home—I don't know when they return home here—or the kingdom comes—but that kingdom will never, never come. So, you keep on going, hoping that somehow you will find some way of achieving your goal. Your interest in attaining that for the purpose of solving your day-to-day problems is a far-fetched idea because that cannot be of any help to you to solve your problems. That is very essential, "If I had that enlighten-ment, I would be able to solve all my problems."

You cannot have all that *and* enlightenment. When that comes, it wipes out everything. You want all this and heaven too. Not a chance! That is something which cannot be made to happen through your effort or through the grace of anybody, through the help of even a god walking on the face of this earth claiming that he has specially descended from wherever, from whatever heavens, for your sake and for the sake of mankind—that is just absolute gibberish. Nobody can help you. Help you to achieve what? That is the question, you see.

As long as your goal is there, so long these persons and their promises and their techniques will look very, very attractive to you. They go together. So it is not *sadhana* that is necessary; there is not something you must do—anyway, you are already doing. So, "Can I be without doing anything?" You can't be without doing anything. Unfortunately you are doing something, and that doing has got to come to an end. In order to bring that doing to come to an end, you are doing something else. That is really the crux of the problem. That's the situation in which you find yourself. That's all that I can say. I point out the absurdity of what you are doing.

As I said yesterday, what brings you here will certainly take you somewhere else. You have nothing to get here; you will not get anything here. Not that I want to keep anything for myself; you can take anything you want. I have nothing to give you. I am not anything that you are not. You think that I am something different. The thought that I am different from others never enters my head. Never. Whenever they ask questions I feel, "Why are these people asking these questions? How can I make them see?" I still have some trace of illusion. Maybe I can try. Even that "try" has no meaning to me. There's nothing that I can do about it.

There is nothing to get—nothing to give and nothing to get. That is the situation. In the material world, yes, we have a lot of things. There is always somebody who can help you with the knowledge, with the money, with so many things in the world. But here in this field there is nothing to give and nothing to get. As long as you want, you can be certain you ain't got a chance. Whatever you want, I am not suggesting you're not getting it, you see, wanting implies that you are going to set in motion thinking to achieve your goal. It is not a question of achieving your goal, but it is a question of this movement coming to an end here. If you want, the only thing that you can do is to set in motion this movement of thought in the direction of achieving that. How are you going to achieve this impossible task?

Wanting and thinking—they always go together. If you don't want a thing—I am not for a moment suggesting that you should suppress all your wants, and free yourself from all your wants, and control all your wants—not at all—that's the religious game. If you want anything, the one thing that you will do is to set in motion the movement of thought to achieve your goal.

Material goals, yes, but even there it's not so easy. It is such a competitive world. Not much is left for us to share, not enough to go around.

Since this is not an experience, the talk of sharing with somebody is poppycock to me. There is nothing to be shared here; it's not an experience. Even assuming for a moment that this is an experience, even then it is so difficult to share with somebody else unless the other individual has some reference point within the framework of his experiencing structure. So, then you see the whole business becomes a sort of meaningless ritual—sitting and discussing these matters. That's all. It's not so easy for you to give up—not at all.

Q: *This thing happened to me when I didn't know anything about anything.*

U.G.: Yes, nothing, you see, it just happened.

Q: *But I just was sitting down on the floor and it happened. I was scared to death about it.*

U.G.: That's all right. Now you want that to happen again, no?

Q: *No, no, because it was not a nice experience at all. But when it happens it's all right.*

U.G.: Yes, but your spiritual search ends that way. There is no other way. It is not that I am frightening you, but how do you expect that to happen? That is how all those people who have taken drugs experience all kinds of things—those who have not heard of anything of this kind suddenly experience so many things and that puts them on this merry-go-round. India has any number of techniques, systems, and methods to give you every kind of experience you want. That is why they are doing a tremendously roaring business.

Q: *But it didn't even come into my head to associate it with meditation, or with this or with that, because it was something different. It was not even me who was...*

U.G.: It happened, such things happen—some extraordinary experiences; people experience without knowing, without asking for that, without doing any such things. This was a frightening experience for you—but you want to make other spiritual experiences happen again and again and again. Anything you make happen has no meaning at all. Then you will want more and more of those things. And then when you succeed in having more and more of those things, you will demand some kind of a permanent situation, permanent happiness, permanent bliss—and there is no such thing as permanence at all.

Q: *It was not bliss at all.*

U.G.: No. Probably it would have resulted in bliss, who knows.

Q: *Are you saying then that we are what we are already?*

U.G.: You don't want to accept that fact, but you want to know what you are. That's the problem. You have no way of knowing it at all. Wanting to know what is there is impossible—that is always related to what you want to be. What you see here is the opposite of what you would like to be, what you want to be, what you ought to be, what you should be. What do you see here? You want to be happy, so you are unhappy. Wanting to be happy creates the unhappiness. What you see here is the opposite of your goal of becoming happy—wanting to be happy. Wanting to have pleasure all the time creates the pain here. So, wanting and thinking, they always go together. They are not separate. Anything you want creates pain, because you begin to think—wanting and thinking—if you don't want a thing in this world, there is no thinking. That does not mean thoughts are not there.

Whether you want to achieve material goals or spiritual goals, it really doesn't matter. I am not saying anything against wanting—wanting means the fulfillment of the want or non-fulfillment of the want is possible only through thinking.

So, the thinking has really created the problem for you. What I am suggesting is that all the problems we have cannot be solved on psychological and ethical levels. Man has tried for centuries to solve them, but he has failed. What keeps him going still is the hope that one day, by doing more and more of the same, he will achieve.

But the body, as I was saying, has a way of resolving these problems, because, you see, it cannot take them. The sensitivity of the sensory perceptions is destroyed by whatever you are doing to free yourself from whatever you want to be free from.

It is destroying the sensitivity of the nervous system here.

The nervous system has to be very alert for the survival of this living organism. It has to be very sensitive. Your sensory perceptions have to be very sensitive. Instead of allowing them to be sensitive, you have invented what is called the "sensitivity" of your feelings; the sensitivity of your mind; the sensitivity towards every living thing around you; sensitivity to the feelings of everybody that is there. And this has created a neurological problem. So all the problems are neurological, not psychological and not ethical. That's the problem of the society.

The society is interested in the status quo; it doesn't want to change. The only way it can maintain the status quo or the continuity is through this demand, the demand that everybody should fit into this structure. Whereas every individual is a unique individual, physically speaking it's a unique individual. Nature is creating something unique all the time. It is not interested in a perfect man; it is not interested in a religious man.

We have placed before man the goal or the ideal of a perfect man, a truly religious man. So anything you do to reach that goal of perfection is destroying the sensitivity of this body; it is creating violence here. It is not interested in that. So the whole thing is set on the wrong way. The dead man, whatever he experienced—self-awareness, self-consciousness—he sowed the seeds of the total destruction of man. All those religions have come out of that divisive consciousness in man. All the teachings of those teachers will inevitably destroy mankind. There is no point in reviving all those things and starting revivalist movements—that is dead, finished.

Anything that is born out of this division in your consciousness is destructive, is violence, because it is trying to protect, not this living organism, not the life, but it is interested in protecting the continuity of thought, and through that it can maintain the status quo of your culture, or whatever you want to call it—the society. The problems are neurological. If you give a chance to the body it will handle all those problems. But if you try to solve them on a psychological level or on an ethical level, you are not going to succeed.

Q: *What do you mean by "giving a chance to the body"?*

UG: Anger is here! Where is anger? In your stomach you feel it, you see, in the base here. So it is handling, but if you beat your husband or wife or neighbor, or beat the pillows, you are not going to solve the problem. It is already absorbed. You are only enriching these therapists who are making money out of that. You hit your wife, husband, anybody you want, and that's all that you can do, nothing else. But still it is the function of the body to handle that and absorb it. It has arisen *here*. It is something real there for the body. It doesn't want this anger, because it is destroying the sensitivity of the nervous system. So, it is absorbing the whole thing, and you don't have to do a thing.

Any energy that you create through this thinking is destructive for this body. That energy cannot be separated from life here. It is one continuous movement. So, all the energies you experience as a result of playing with all those things are not of any interest to the smooth functioning of this living organism. It is disturbing the very harmonious functioning of this body—it is a very, very peaceful thing.

The peace there is not this innate dead silence you experience. But it's like a volcano erupting all the time. That is the silence; that is peace. The blood is flowing through your veins like a river. If you try to magnify the sound of the flow of your blood you will be surprised—it's like the roar of the ocean. If you put yourself in a soundproof room you will not survive even for five minutes. You will go crazy, because you can't bear the noises that are there in you. The beat of your heart is something that you cannot take. You love to surround yourself with all these sounds and then you create some funny experience called "the experience of the silent mind," which is ridiculous—absurd. That is the silence that is there, the roar, the roar of an ocean; like the roaring of the flow of blood.

That is all that it is interested in, not your state of mind nor the experience of the silent mind. It's not interested in your practice of virtues; not interested in the practice of your silences. The body has no interest in your moral dilemma or whatever you want to call it—moral problems. It's not interested in your virtues or vices. As long as you practice virtues, so long you will remain a man of vice. They go together. If you are lucky enough to be free from this pursuit of virtue, as a goal, along with it the vice also goes out of your system. You will not remain a man of vice. You will not remain a man of violence. As long as you follow some idea of becoming a non-violent, kind, soft, gentle person, so long you will remain the opposite. A kind man, a man who is practicing kindness, a man who is practicing virtues is really the menace—not the violent man. Both are!

Somewhere along the line, culture has put the whole thing on the wrong track by placing before man the ideal of a perfect man, the ideal of a truly religious man, because the religious experience is born out of this division in his consciousness, which is not its nature.

Luckily the animals don't have this division in their consciousness, except the division that is essential for the survival of those animals. Man is worse than an animal. He has no doubt succeeded in putting man on the moon, probably he will put men on every planet, but that achievement is of no interest to this body. That achievement is progressively moving in the direction of destroying everything, because anything that is born out of thought is destructive, not only destructive to the body, but progressively destructive in destroying everything that man has built for himself.

Q: *Anything is destructive if you are hungry.*

U.G.: Your body is not interested in your hunger after one day. You will be surprised if you don't feed the body. Feeding your body is your own problem. Maybe for one or two days you will feel the hunger tantrums.

Q: *Yeah, but if you never eat anymore, you will die.*

U.G.: So what. The body doesn't die. It changes its form, shape, breaks itself into its constituent elements. It is not interested in that. For the body there is no death. For your thinking there is a death, because it does not want to come to an end. For the thought there is a death. It does not want to face that situation, so it has created the life after, the lives to come. But this body is immortal in its nature, because this is part of life.

Q: *Even when the body is under the ground and disintegrating?*

U.G.: So what? There are so many other forms of life surviving on that body. It is of no consolation to you, but all those germs will have a heyday on your body—a feast day, a big feast! If you leave the body there in the streets, like the dog, you will be surprised. They will all have a field day, a feast. You will be doing great service; not for mankind, but for organisms of different kinds.

Q: *It is also not advisable to be a vegetarian?*

U.G.: Ah, well. (*U.G. sighs wearily.*)

Q: *Here we go again.*

U.G.: Vegetarianism for what, for some spiritual goals? One

70

form of life lives off another; that's a fact, whether you like it or not. If tigers practiced vegetarianism... He says his cat is a vegetarian cat, it doesn't kill a fly, because of its association with vegetarians it has become vegetarian, maybe. For health reasons maybe one should—I don't know, I don't see any adequate reason why one should be a vegetarian. Your body is not going to be any more pure than the meat-eating body. You go to India, those that have been vegetarians, they are not kind, they are not peaceful. So it has nothing to do... what you put in there is not really the problem.

Q: *What about aggression, which is caused by eating meat?*

U.G.: Vegetarians are more aggressive than the meat eaters. You will be surprised. You read the history of India—bloodshed, massacres, and assassinations in the name of religion.

Buddhism has not been as violent in some areas, but it was the most violent religion when it spread to Japan. Even Buddhism—those temples maintained armies and provided arms to fight battles in Japan. That's history, not my personal opinion.

That's why I am saying, emphasizing that the teachers and the teachings are responsible for this mess in this world. All those messiahs have created nothing but a mess in this world. And the politicians are the inheritors of that culture. There is no use blaming them and calling them corrupt. They were corrupt—the man who taught love was corrupt because he created division in his consciousness—who talked of "Love thy neighbor as thyself" was responsible for this horror in the world today—if you want to call this a horror. Don't exonerate those teachers. Their teachings have created nothing but a mess in this world, progressively moving in the direction of destroying not only man, but every kind of species on this planet today. So it came out of that—it's not the scientists, not the politicians that are responsible. Luckily they have this power in their hands, and they are going to use it—there are enough lunatics in this world that will press the button. But it originated where?

Religion is not going to save man, nor atheism, nor communism, nor any of those systems. They are all the religions. It originated there. You can't put them on a pedestal and say that they should be exonerated. Not only the teachings, but the teachers themselves have sown the seeds of this violence that we have in this world. The man who talked of love is responsible, because love and hate go together. So how can you exonerate them? Don't blame the followers; the followers have come out of that teaching. That's history, not my personal opinion—you know the history of Europe. The inquisitions, "in the name of Jesus." Why do you want to revive that religion? What for? "Back to Christianity" is the slogan now everywhere. I am not condemning any particular thing. *All* are responsible for that.

Talk of love is one of the most absurd things—there must be two. Wherever there is a division there is this destruction. Kindness needs two—you are kind to somebody, or you are kind to yourself. There is a division there in your consciousness. Anything that is born out of that division is a protective mechanism, and in the long run it is destructive.

Q: *Protective against what?*

U.G.: It is trying to protect itself—thought is protecting itself. That is why it is interested in continuity. The body is not interested in protecting itself. Whatever intelligence is necessary for the survival of the body is already there. The jungle we have created through our organization needs that intellect, the intellect that we have acquired through our studies, through our culture, through the whole lot. It has a parallel existence of its own and it is interested in a survival of a different kind, because there is no end to the life here.

This is only an expression of the life—if you and I go, the life goes on. Those lights go off, but the electricity continues. Something else will come. It is not interested in man. Man, unfortunately, has such destructive power, which has resulted out of the original experience of man—the self-awareness.

So the whole talk of wanting to look at himself, to understand himself, is a divisive movement in man, born out of that self-awareness. That's the foundation on which the whole psychological structure is built.

Q: *But how can we get rid of that divisive thinking?*

U.G.: You can't. It's not in your hands; anything you do adds momentum to that. So do you want that to come to an end? No.

Q: *I once felt an enormous unity...*

U.G.: That's what they feel also, you know, when they do meditation, when they do vipassana—oneness—a disturbance in the metabolism of the body, brought about through drugs or through meditation or through any of those systems and techniques man has invented. You can experience the oneness of life, the unity of life—and look at India, which preached the unity of life and the oneness of life—there you have an example. They talk, you know, they are all great metaphysicians, philosophers, everlastingly discussing these things, but it doesn't operate in the lives of the people.

Q: *The understanding that there is that dualism, the coming of that understanding...*

U.G.: Understanding is dualism. If that division is not there, there is nothing to understand. So the instrument, which you are using to understand something, is the only instrument

73

you have. There is no other instrument. You can talk of intuition; you can talk of a thousand other things; they are all sensitized thoughts. The intuition is nothing but a sensitized thought—but still it is a thought.

So, anything you understand through the help of that instrument has not helped you to understand anything. That is not the instrument, and there is no other instrument. If that is the case, is there anything to understand? Your understanding anything is only for the purpose of changing what is there. Whatever is there, you want to change. So by understanding this, you want to bring about a change—change not what is there, but change in the structure of your thinking. So, you begin to think differently, and you begin to experience differently. But basically there is no change there.

So, your wanting to understand anything is only for the purpose of bringing about a change there, and at the same time you do not want the change. That has created the neurotic situation in man, wanting two things, change and no change. That is the conflict that is there all the time.

Q: *Is it possible to see that conflict through some kind of other method than thinking?*

U.G.: The seeing itself is a divisive movement—there are two things. You know, the Indians are past masters in this game—the seer and the seen, the observer and the observed. They are great experts in this kind of a game. But what is there to see? Who is it that is seeing? Are there two things? What do you do when you see? You are back again to the same thought.

* * * * * * *

It is absurd, you see, to talk of posing to yourself the question of "Who am I?" That has become the basic teaching of *Ramana Maharshi*. "Who am I?" Why do you ask that question—who am I? That means there is some other "I" there, which you want to know. That question to me has no meaning at all. The very fact that you ask that question, "Who am I," implies that there are two things. The "I" you know, and there is another "I" the nature of which you do not know. So you are better off asking the question, and getting an answer, if you can, about what you know. The question "Who am I" implies that there is some other "I", the nature of which you really do not know and you want to know. I don't know if I make myself clear. Do you know anything about yourself, first of all? What do you know? Tell me. Hm?

Q: *What he knows.*

U.G.: What he has been told—where he lives; what his name is; how much money he is drawing every month; and his telephone number; how many people he has met; how many experiences he has gathered during the course of his 30 years—that's all that he can tell you—all the books he has read—he can repeat mechanically all the information he has gathered and all the experiences he has collected, and so that is all that is there. Why are you dissatisfied with it, and why are you searching for something other than that? Can you tell me something about yourself other than the information that you gathered, what you know?

Q: *Yes, what I found there is not the answer. Otherwise the questions would not persist.*

U.G.: What did you find there?

Q: *Just knowledge.*

U.G.: So that question, that idiotic question, is born out of the knowledge you already have. So this is the knowledge that is there that has thrown out this question, "Who am I?" So you want to know, and through that knowing the knowledge you have gathers momentum—you are adding more and more and more. If there is anything to be known there, all you know should come to an end. So, by this pursuit, or the demand to get an answer for that question, you are adding more and more to the knowledge.

So, don't you see the absurdity of the question, "Who am I?" It doesn't matter who suggested that, who threw that question at you, who recommended that question. There is nothing there to know. What is there is all that you know. When that is not there, there is no need for you to know, and there is no way of knowing anything about what is there.

Q: *But "Who am I" is not really a question.*

U.G.: A statement.

Q: *"Who am I" is a pointer.*

U.G.: Yes. Where does it lead you, the pointer? All right, if it is a pointer, what do you do? You stay put there and instead of following that, you suck the finger. I am not trying to be rude or anything. What do you do with that pointer?

Q: *The pointer points to where there is nothing to be pointed. "Who am I" takes you — these are all nonsensical words.*

U.G.: That's all right; the question itself is a nonsensical question.

Q: *Yes. But it is only so if you use it as a question.*

U.G.: All right, even if you use it as a pointer, the very direction is wrong.

Q: *It's not even a pointer.*

U.G.: All right, what is it then?

Q: *It shows you that you are. It shows you that I am. "I am" is the basis.*

U.G.: What I am is the knowledge I have about myself.

Q: *"I am" is what I am.*

U.G.: But what does it mean, "What I am?"

Q: *It doesn't actually mean anything...*

U.G.: Yes.

Q: *"I am" is not knowledge.*

U.G.: There is nothing there, no existence there independent of the question.

Q: *So it is the end of knowledge.*

U.G.: So the question should end. Because the question itself—listen—the question itself is born out of the answer. Otherwise, there is no place for any question of any kind. All questions are born out of the answers you already have. So, it is idiotic even to ask a question for which you already have an answer. Because there can't be any question without an answer. The question implies that there is something about that "I" you do not know, or you want to know—something other than the "I" that is already there—that there is another "I".

Q: *On a certain level, yes, you can also say if you ask a question it means that you know the answer.*

U.G.: That's right. There's no question at all. There can't be any question without knowledge. All questions are born out of the answers you already have. So, that is the reason why a question of that kind, whether it is posed by yourself or somebody else, does not want an answer for that question. The answer for any question is the end of the question. The end of the question means the end of the answer that you already have. Not only your answer, the answers that have been accumulating for centuries mustn't be there. The demand for an answer to that question, on any level (there is only one level, there are no other levels), implies that the questioner does not want the knowledge to come to an end.

Q: *Quite so, that's true. But of course in the process of this...*

U.G.: That has to happen now, not in the end, because there is no time. The instrument you are using, which is this process of knowledge, does not want to come to an end. That is why it is posing the question to itself, knowing very well that the question is bound to carry on until it gets an answer.

So, this knowledge, the instrument that you are using, does not know or cannot conceive of the possibility of anything happening except in time, because it is born in time and it functions in time. Although it projects a state of timelessness, it is not interested in accepting the fact that nothing can happen except in the field of time. The question implies that there is a demand for an answer and that the answer can come only in time—and during that time, this has a chance of survival.

Q: *It's true what you say. However, the answer to the question "Who am I" does not fall in time.*

U.G.: Yes. But anything that is born ...

Q: *It is only a device. I agree with you.*

U.G.: That is true. Anything that is born in the field of time *is* time. The question *is* time.

Q: *The question is not born in time.*

U.G.: Well then, where does it come from?

Q: *It comes from "I am."*

U.G.: That assumption itself is time—that, "I am."

Q: *But "I am" is not an assumption.*

U.G.: Of course it is an assumption that there is something there other than this knowledge. What is there is only the knowledge.

Q: *If, as you say, you ask questions born out of the answers you already have, do you mean that "the answers that you already have" is the same as perhaps what psychology means by the "mind"?*

U.G.: I don't know... to me there is no mind at all. The mind is the totality. It's not that I am giving a peculiar definition of mind—the totality of your experiences and the totality of your thoughts. As I was saying yesterday, there are no thoughts which you can call your own; there are no experiences which you can call your own. Without knowledge you cannot have any experience. I don't know if I make myself clear.

Every time you experience, through the help of this knowledge, the knowledge is strengthened and fortified. This is a vicious circle. It goes on and on and on and on. The knowledge gives you experiences and the experiences fortify the knowledge you have.

The questions, which you are asking, are very frivolous questions, because the questions are born out of the knowledge. If there is any answer to that question, it is not necessarily your answer—the answers that have been accumulating through centuries. So there is a totality of the knowledge that has been accumulating—cumulative knowledge, cumulative experiences are there. You are using them to communicate to yourself and to communicate to others. So, there is no such thing as your mind and my mind, but there is a mind, which is the totality of all the thoughts and experiences of all that has existed up to this point. I don't know if I make myself clear.

So, any answer that anybody gives for that question should put an end to that question. The fact is that the answers given by others, and the answers that you have manufactured for yourself, or the answers given by these wise men we have around us in the marketplace today, and those who existed in the past (let's not bother about those who existed in the past), are not really the answers. So, any answer I give to your question cannot be the answer for that question, because the answer should put an end to the question. If the question is shattered there, along with it all the knowledge that is responsible for that question has also got to go. I don't know if I make myself clear.

The questioner is not interested in any answer, because the answer has to blow up the whole thing, not only what little you have known in these 30 or 40 years, but all that has accumulated up to that point, everything that every man thought and felt and experienced before, up to the point where the question is thrown out. I don't think I am making myself clear. But anyway, you see, the answer, if there is any answer, should wipe out the whole thing.

Q: *I was thinking of the despair that occurs when the vacuum is on the brink of becoming a reality, or seemingly near.*

U.G.: Yes, but, assuming for a moment that there is despair there—you say you are in great despair—have you given up trying to free yourself from despair? You call it despair, like the way you are using the word vacuum or emptiness, but there is no despair there, because there is a movement in the direction of wanting to be free from that situation you call despair. Just the way the existentialist philosophers have built up a tremendous philosophical structure on what they call "despair," or the religious people call it the "divine despair"—these are all meaningless phrases.

You have never come to grips with what you call despair, because there is already a movement in the direction of wanting somehow to free yourself from the situation which you call despair. So you don't let that despair act. That is the action that I am talking about.

Where is that despair? It is not in the area of your thinking. It should be here in the framework of your body. So where is that despair you are talking about? As long as you are trying to run away, move away from the despair, there is no despair there.

So, wanting to be free from despair is all that you are interested in, because it is not choking you; it is not killing you. The despair should destroy this movement for freeing yourself from despair. You are not giving a chance for the despair to act. You are interested in finding out a solution, a way out of this impasse. That's all that is there, and you give it a name and call it "despair." You are not in despair. You don't act like a person in despair. You just talk about despair, you talk about vacuum, and you talk about emptiness. It's not really emptiness—if there is emptiness, that's the action of life.

Then you will ask me "What is life?" If I define life, we are lost. It's one definition against life. What exactly I mean by "life" is that which makes it possible for the whole of your being to respond—not react to the situation, respond—respond to the stimuli around you. If there is no life there you become a corpse—a dead corpse. A dead corpse cannot respond the way the living body is responding, but it is still responding in a different way. That is why you call this "life." Life, in other words, is nothing but the pulse and the beat and the breath of life. That's also a definition. There is a pulse, there is breathing, there is a throb of life. It is throbbing all over, everywhere; every cell in your body is throbbing. That's all that is life.

So if we give a definition ... But we are not really talking about that life, because nobody can say anything about that life, except to give definitions. You can call it life force, this, that and the other, but the living implies all the other problems that the so-called living creates.

So, there is a demand for "how." How to live—that is really the problem. The problem of all the problems is how to live. And for centuries we have been brainwashed that, "This is how you should live." If that is not satisfactory, you find another way and call that, "How to live." And it goes on and on and on and on. All that may be nonsense, because it has not given you peace. All the time there is a constant battle going on inside of you, a war going on inside of you. As long as there is a war inside of you, there isn't going to be a peaceful world at all. Even assuming for a moment that war has come to an end, and you are at peace with yourself, that will not change anything, because, you see, a man who is at peace with himself will be a threat to his neighbor. So, there is a danger that he will liquidate you.

The important problem is, can you bring this war to an end within yourself—is there any way? All the solutions that you have are the ones that are responsible for this battle that is going on, "How to live." The "how" has to go. So then you ask me, "How can that 'how' go? Can you help me?"

First of all, you are not sure of that. You have not even come to that point that there is despair. Only then can you deal with the despair. As long as you are moving away, running in the direction of wanting to be free from despair, it is just not possible for you to handle that. That's all that I am saying.

So that is the reason I say that is the problem—you don't look for solutions. There may be a hundred and fifty solutions, but you can't try all of them. Obviously all that you have tried has failed, and so you say you are in despair.

That despair will act. That's all that I am saying—what is the action? That action can never be within the framework of your thinking. Any action that is within the framework or the product of your thinking will inevitably create despair. It may give you certain reasons for a while, or certain experiences, but you always demand more and more and more of the same. And then, you see, this keeps the whole thing going, and then that gives you hope.

The hope is here, and you say the situation is hopeless. The situation is not hopeless. The hope is here now because, as you say, the despair is there. And so the hope to resolve that, to solve that, to handle that, to come to grips with it, and find out if there is any way of freeing yourself from the despair—instead of letting that act, you are running away from it and still trying to find out if there is any way that you can be free from the despair.

That applies to all the situations in life. Either you are stuck with your frustration, which is despair, or something else. What do you want to do in such a situation? You have to find out the solution for yourself. If I give you another solution it will be like the hundreds of solutions that you already have. You will add this to the list of solutions that you have. This is not going to help you to solve your problem. That makes it more difficult—one more solution you have. If there is any solution, that solution has to come from that which you are trying to be free from, and not from any outside agency. That is going to act—that action is something extraordinary.

If once that problem of despair is solved, all the others are solved, because every other problem is a variation of the same. So you never want to solve the problem. You are more interested in solutions. That's why I am repeating the same thing over and over in ten different words. My vocabulary is limited so I have to use the same words. You can increase your vocabulary and find new phrases, but it doesn't serve any purpose.

The instrument you are using, which is thinking, can never accept the fact that these problems can be solved here and now, because that has come into being through years—so much time it has taken for you to be what you are. You are living in a world of your experiences and it has taken so many years for you to be what you are. That is the only instrument you have. You have no other way of handling these problems. So that cannot conceive of the possibility of finding out a solution here and now. It is always interested in pushing it further and further and further away—there is always tomorrow, there is always this time. Because this functions in the field of time, it cannot conceive of the possibility of anything happening, of any action other than the action in the field of time. This is not metaphysics that I am discussing.

The solution, if there is any, has to be here and now. If you are hungry, hunger must be satisfied. If the hunger cannot be satisfied, it will burn you out. This is a frightening situation for you, so you are satisfied with the crumbs, which are the solutions that people throw at you, or you are waiting for somebody to give you a full loaf of bread or some miracle man to multiply the loaves of bread. That's not going to happen even then, but you can't wait until then. There is no real hunger there. You don't want to solve this problem, because then you will find yourself without a problem. So, what gives you strength, energy, is trying to solve your problem. This happens always—when once you achieve your goal, what you have there is frustration.

Even in the sex act, which is so powerful in the life of an individual, it is the preparation, it is the build-up; it is the tension that is the attractive part of it. When once the tension is built up there, this body is demanding release from the tension which you call pleasure. Release—it wants to be released from the tension, which you have built up. It wants a release, which you call the orgasm, or whatever you want to call it. So there is a tremendous relief.

So, what is there now? The vacuum. So in exactly the same way, all actions are functioning in the same field. You build up, build up, build up tension, and then you see it demands a release from the tensions.

So all these therapies that man has invented are really not going to solve anything. The other day I was reading an article in *Playboy*, "How to Keep The Orgasm Going for Half an Hour." Oh my God! They are doing experiments. You know they have succeeded. There was one doctor in California who has succeeded in that, where no man can help the woman, but through artificial means, with the help of gadgets, they have established the fact that a woman can have an orgasm for half an hour. All the other specialists say it's only for a few seconds. But why I mentioned that is, the demand for the extension of that agony, which you call pleasure, is not pleasure, it is tension.

You work hard to achieve your goal, and once you achieve the goal you are exhausted, you are finished, the charm is lost for you. Working for it, building up all these tensions—that is all that you are interested in. When once you are there, it's finished for you. You have lost it. So you start all over again.

You don't want to be without any problems. You are yourself the problem. If you don't have any problems, you create problems. The end of the problem is the end of you, so these problems will remain until the end. If you go, then the problems go. Seventy, eighty, ninety, a hundred years—it depends upon how long you are going to live—the hope remains. It's not a pessimistic situation; it's really a realistic situation. I am not giving you any solutions. Please, for goodness' sake, look at your problem if you can. You can't separate yourself from the problem—that's really the problem—and say, "This is the problem." The problem is created by the opposite of it.

Why do you feel unhappy, first of all? Why do you feel this feeling of unkindness in you? Because of the goal, which creates the opposite. You can see for yourself, I don't have to tell you—"I should be like that; I ought to be like that; I must be like that," and yet "I am not like that." If that goal is gone, this opposite also is gone. If that is gone, this also is gone. This man cannot be a cruel man. This man cannot be an insensitive man—not sensitive within the framework of your cultural mores.

This is a different kind of sensitivity. As long as you are pursuing those ideals that the society or the culture has placed before you, so long you will remain the opposite of it. And you hope that one day, through some miracle or through the help of somebody, some god, some guru, you will be able to resolve the problem. Not a chance!

I cannot create the hunger in you. How can I create the hunger in you? If you have a hunger, you will look around and you will find that whatever is offered to you is not satisfying. If you are satisfied with the crumbs, all right, that's what the gurus are doing, throwing some crumbs at you, like the dog on a leash. Humans are like animals, no difference. If we accept the fact that we are not different, then there is a better chance that we will act as humans.

Q: *When will they act as humans?*

U.G.: When man ceases to pursue the goal of a perfect man.

Part III

Nice Meeting You, And Goodbye!

Q: *May I ask you something?*

U.G.: Yes, please.

Q: *This constant change that we want to come about with our inner self, not necessarily changing the world but trying to find our inner self when we do meditation or yoga or we do whatever we feel, why do we want this change?*

U.G.: Why do you do them all?

Q: *Well I try them out, I do them, and I see if they make me feel better — yoga and...*

U.G.: What for do you do? You want to change something.

Q: *That's the point, yes. Why do we want to change? What is it in us that wants this constant change? Why can't we be satisfied?*

U.G.: You are dissatisfied with yourself, first of all. Hm?

Q: *Not consciously — it's a funny thing. I feel very good; I have relatively little to complain about. I pride myself on that point, and yet I...*

U.G.: And yet you do ... Do you see the paradox? You are not as contented as you say you are, as satisfied as you say you are.

Q: *That's right.*

U.G.: Something there demands that all is not right there. That's why you want to bring about a change. And who is responsible for that demand to change? That is what I am saying, the culture, the society has placed before you the demand that you should be like that, you ought to be like that. So you have accepted that as a model for yourself.

Q: *But I don't feel that I have that. I am not looking... I don't have an image of a person or a thing that I feel that this is what I am striving for. What I am trying to find is whether there is something more inside.*

U.G.: No. The demand for more...

Q: *Yeah, more inside — the inner thing...*

U.G.: No, there is no inner and outer. What I am trying to say is that there is a feeling, there is a demand that there is something more interesting that you can do with yourself, more meaningful, more purposeful than your existence is today. That is the demand, you see. That is why there is this restlessness. You become restless because of this drive in you, which is put in there by the society or culture, that makes you feel that there is something more interesting, more meaningful, more purposeful that your life can be, than what it is today.

Q: *And trying to find the naturalness of your self doesn't exist?*

U.G.: No.

Q: *It's just words that the society has put together.*

U.G.: Exactly. Your naturalness is destroyed by that demand which is put in there by the culture. So then your life looks meaningless to you—if that is all that you can do—you have tried to fill in that boredom with everything possible. Now you have all these new gimmicks—yoga, meditation and all the psychology.

Q: *Reading books...*

U.G.: Reading books, religious books—this is something new added on to the already existing things there, but you have not succeeded in freeing yourself from the boredom. That is the demand.

Q: *You have to have something to do.*

U.G.: You are bored with your life, with your existence, because it's very repetitive. First of all, your physical needs are very well taken care of, here in this part of the world at least. So, there is no need for you to spend any more energy to survive. That part is taken care of.

When that is taken care of, the natural question that arises is a very simple question: "Is that all that is there?" Going to the office every morning, or just being a house-wife doing all the chores of the house, or sleeping, having sex—everything, you see—is that all? It is that demand on your part that is being exploited by these holy men—"Is that all?" So, those are some of the gimmicks that you use to try to fill the boredom there.

It's an empty, bottomless cup—it's not even a bottomless cup, it is a bottomless pit. You can fill that all the time with every conceivable thing that you can imagine or that others can come up with, but yet the boredom is a reality; it's a fact. Sure, otherwise, you wouldn't do anything. You are just bored, simply bored with doing the same thing again and again and again, and you don't see any meaning in this.

Q: *You're not quite conscious of that boredom.*

U.G.: Not quite conscious of that boredom, because you are looking for something to free you from what is not there. That's all that I have been emphasizing all the time. The problem is not really the boredom. You are not conscious of the existence of boredom either on the conscious level of your thinking or even on the unconscious level of your existence.

The attractiveness of those things to free you from the non-existing boredom has really created the boredom, and those things really cannot fill this boredom created by that. So it goes on and on and on and on—the newer and newer and newer techniques and methods—every year we have a new guru coming from India with a new gimmick, with a new technique or some new therapy, you know—all kinds of things.

Q: *All right, then when we talk about consciousness?*

U.G.: Yes, yes, I know. You seem to know something about consciousness. Will you please tell me what exactly do you mean by consciousness?

Q: *I don't know. I was going to ask you that question.*

U.G.: Why are you asking me the question about conscious-ness? I am not throwing a counter-question at you. You have picked up that word somewhere, you see. You have picked that up somewhere, and so they are talking of expanding consciousness ...

Q: *...in the form of trying to get to know oneself better, trying to find the naturalness that society talks about — the naturalness of the human being.*

U.G.: The naturalness of your self is something that you don't have to know. You just have to let that function in its own way. Do you understand? So, your wanting to *know* that demands some know-how, which you want from somebody. The functioning of the heart is a natural thing; the functioning of all the organs in your body is very natural. They are not for one moment asking themselves the question, "How am I functioning?" The whole living organism has this tremendous intelligence, which makes it function in a very natural way. You have certain ideas of how that should act. You have separated what you call "life" from that. What you call life is living, which is in no way related to the functioning of this living organism.

So, naturally, you are asking the question, "How to live?" How to live is your problem. You are looking for answers for how to live. You see, it is "How to live" that has really destroyed the natural way the whole thing is going on. That is where the culture steps in and says, "This is the way you should act. This is the way you should live. This is the one and the only thing that is good for you and good for the society." You want to change that, you see—something there—what is it that you want to change there? That is all that I am asking.

Q: *I wish I knew.*

U.G.: You will never know. So, what is it that you are trying now then? Don't you see the absurdity of what you are doing?

93

Q.: *In a way, yes.*

U.G.: All this searching is like trying to chase something that does not exist at all.

I always give my pet simile. We all take it for granted that there is such a thing as a horizon there. So, if you look at that and say, "That is a horizon," it sounds very simple to you. But you forget that the physical limitation, the limitation of your physical eye, fixes on that point there and it calls it "horizon." So you are moving in the direction of the horizon, and the more you move in that direction, the faster you move in the direction, with the aid of all these mechanical means, like supersonic planes, the more it is moving farther and farther and farther away. So instead of finding out what it is that is limiting your physical capacity to see, instead of bothering your head, breaking your head over that—capturing that—then you will be able to understand the limitations of this, and not bother about that. It doesn't exist at all. What you are stuck with is only the limitation.

I give also another example of trying to overtake your shadow. As children we always played this game of trying to overtake our shadows—all the other boys running with you, everybody trying to overtake his own shadow. It never occurred to us then that it is this body that is casting this shadow there, and your wanting to overtake that shadow is an absurd game that you are playing. You can run for miles and miles and miles.

You know the story of Alice in Wonderland. The Red Queen has to run faster and faster and faster in order to keep still where she is. You see that's exactly what you are all doing—running faster and faster and faster, but you are not moving anywhere—you are doing all that to find out exactly where you are. This is not moving at all. That gives you the feeling that you are working on something, you are doing something to achieve your goal, not knowing very well that what you are doing is totally unrelated to the natural functioning of this body, and you want to act in a natural way. You are not acting in a natural way, because the ideal you have placed before you, and which you have accepted, placed before you by the culture, has falsified the natural actions here. You are frightened of acting in a very natural way, because you have been told that this is the way you should act, you ought to act.

Physical perfection is one of the means. I am not saying anything against yoga. Please don't get me wrong. I am not saying anything against meditation—do meditation, do yoga—they are all certain palliatives. If you want to keep your body supple, do it. A supple body is better than a stiff body. That's all right. So you see, instead of creating tensions all the time, if meditation gives you relief from your tensions—do it. But I am suggesting that it is the meditation that is creating all the tensions. You first create the problem, and then you try to solve the problem. It's all right, but thank god you are not doing it very seriously. That's the only hope you have.

If you very seriously meditate, you are in trouble. You will go crazy. Or, if you try to practice this awareness all the time—in your conscious as well as unconscious levels—you will be really in trouble. You will end up in the loony bin, singing loony tunes and merry melodies.

Q: *Oh, thank you!*

U.G.: Now you can learn the new songs from India—Hare Krishna songs, and sing and enjoy. That's all right, but don't do that because it's something like trying to walk while watching every step you take. You will be in trouble; you will not be able to walk at all. So don't do that. It's a mechanical thing—the things that are there are running very smoothly and mechanically. You don't have to do a thing about them.

The more you try to do it, the more resistance you are creating.

The boredom is really the problem for you. The non-existing boredom has been created by the demand, "How to free yourself from boredom." Since that is not in any way helping you to be free from your boredom, but making it more and more and more difficult to be free from this, you have to shop around. You have to search for all and every kind of gimmick to free yourself from that non-existing boredom. So it is that which is keeping this going on forever and ever.

I am not giving you another gimmick or suggesting anything. I just want you to look at this, what you are doing to yourself—not to free you from something and take you away from that because I have some new product to sell—not at all. I have no new products to sell, nor am I interested in selling anything. We just happen to be here, all of us, for some reason or the other—I don't know why we are here, but anyway we are here, so we might as well … Not even the exchanging of ideas, that is meaningless—or discussion—there is nothing to discuss here.

The discussion has no meaning, because the object or the purpose of a discussion or a conversation is to understand something. So, that is not the means to understand anything. Ultimately, what I am emphasizing all the time is, "Look here, there is nothing to understand." When that is understood, that there is nothing to understand, all these conversations become meaningless. So you get up and walk away once and for all. So I say, "Nice meeting you, and good-bye."

That's all that I am saying all the time, "Nice meeting you, and goodbye."

Q: *We just don't understand it.*

U.G.: No, that's exactly what I am saying all the time, "Nice meeting you, and goodbye. God be with you and stay with God." That's the Spanish—stay with God. Your God, your gurus—stay with them, you see. Don't disturb yourself unnecessarily. Live in hope and die in hope. And hope that you will be born again, if you accept the theory of reincarnation and all that. One birth is bad enough. Why would we want to be born again? We might as well handle this problem once and for all, now, and begin to live—what little is left for us. Don't bother about the world and the peace of the world.

If the question of how to be happy is dropped, then you begin to live, you see, not bothering about happiness at all. That doesn't exist; happiness doesn't exist at all. The more you want it, the more you search for it, the more unhappy you remain. They go together, you see.

Q: *Maybe I will ask a question to somebody else here: do people who listen to you much longer than I have...*

U.G.: That's enough.

Q.: *Don't you think that it goes against everything about religion, society...*

U.G.: Culture.

Q.: *Culture...*

U.G.: All systems of thought.

Q: *Structures, systems, all systems...*

U.G.: All structures of thought, philosophical, religious, materialistic structures...

Q: *Don't you think that's negative? Not just because I think it's negative, but people would say…*

U.G.: Why are you saying it is negative? Listen…

Q: *… because people say that, not me, but people.*

U.G.: People can say that because it's an easy way out for them. You forget one thing—all the positive approaches that man has invented and used for centuries, have not resulted in any useful way. They have not produced the results you have been promised. And yet you go on and on and on, hoping that somehow, through some miracle, you will be able to achieve your positive goals, or the goals that are placed before us through the positive approach. You keep doing it only because you have hope, and it is that hope that keeps you going. Then somebody presents the other side of it: look, don't be caught up in the structure of thought, which always suggests the positive and negative. Your goals are always positive. Since your goals have failed to give the desired results, you have begun to look at these things and approach them in a negative way. The positive and negative approaches function only in the field of thought.

What I am suggesting is, look, your positive approach so far has not given you the desired results, and I am telling you why it has not given you the desired results. I am telling you why you are stuck where you are stuck. But immediately you turn around and say, "Your approach is negative." It is not at all negative. I am presenting the other side of the coin, or the other side of the picture, to neutralize your argument, not to win you over to my point of view, or to stress the negative approach to the problems. Your goal being a positive goal—no matter what approach you adopt, it is a positive approach. You may call it a negative approach, but it is still a positive approach.

So, you must be very, very clear about the goal. What I am trying to emphasize is that the goal must go.

Q: *You leave the goal?*

U.G.: It has no meaning at all. The goal has no meaning. The goal which they have placed before you has no meaning at all, because it has resulted only in struggle, pain and sorrow for you.

You are using will, as I said a while ago, and the will has certain limitations, you can't use it beyond a certain limit. The use of your will and the use of your effort gives you a sort of additional energy to tackle these problems and to face these problems, but actually it is limited in its scope. The energy that you produce is only a frictional energy. The will creates a friction, and that friction gives you some sort of energy, but that energy cannot last long, and so you are back again in square one.

Q: *I think you also realize that the whole Western, Christian civilization is built upon the goal.*

U.G.: Why Western civilization? All civilizations, all cultures place before you a goal, whether it is a material goal or a spiritual goal. There are ways and means of achieving your material goals, but even in this respect there is a lot of pain, there is a lot of suffering, and you have superimposed on that what is called a "spiritual goal".

Christianity, for example, is built on the foundation of suffering as a means to reach your goal. What you are left with is only the suffering, and you make a great big thing out of suffering, and yet you are not anywhere near the goal, whatever is the nature of your goal. In the material world the goal is something tangible. The instrument, which you are using to achieve your material goal, does produce

99

certain results. By using that more and more you have a way of achieving the desired results, but there is no guarantee.

The instrument that you are using is limited in its scope; it is applicable only in this area. So, the instrument, which you are using to achieve your so-called spiritual goals, is the same instrument. You do not realize that the spiritual goals that are superimposed on your so-called material goals are born out of your fantasy, because you have divided life into material and spiritual. It doesn't matter what instrument you use to achieve your goal, whether it is material or spiritual, it is exactly the same.

Q: *Is it not so that we as human beings are active persons? We are not plants. Even plants are active, living beings. We are not passive. We must have some sort of a goal. Are you saying that it is bad to have a goal?*

U.G.: I am not saying that. I want you to be very clear about the goal. What do you want?

Q.: *The type of goal?*

U.G.: What do you want? It is not the want that is wrong, but the only way you can achieve your material or spiritual goals is through the instrument that you use to achieve your goal, to reach your goal, to attain your goal. What I am suggesting is that the only instrument you have is through thinking.

See, "I want to be a millionaire." A millionaire wants to be a billionaire, and a billionaire wants to be a trillionaire. So, that is the goal. A happy man would never want to be happy—he wants to be more and more happy, or he wants to be permanently happy—sure. You are happy sometimes and you are unhappy some other times; you want pleasures and you want those pleasures to be permanent, and at the same time, you also know that the so-called demand for pleasure, temporary or otherwise, is giving you pain as well. The goal of every person in this world—whether here in the West or in the East or even in communist countries—is exactly the same. He wants is to have pleasure without pain at all, and to be happy always, even without moments of unhappiness. What he is actually struggling and striving hard for is to achieve this impossible goal of having one without the other.

Q: *But that isn't true of older people.*

U.G.: Everybody.

Q: *But older people know that there is no pleasure without pain. There is no luck without bad luck, because you cannot speak of luck if you don't know what bad luck is. Older people know that everybody gets his portion of bad luck and suffering. And those people are not thinking of getting pleasure without pain. They know they get pain.*

U.G.: And yet, you see, they want to make it possible to be without pain—sure. That's all that I am saying. Whether they are consciously doing it or not, that is what everybody is after. You know what will give you happiness.

Q: *Paradise.*

U.G.: If you achieve all the goals you have placed before yourself, the success, the money, the name and the fame, position or power, you are happy. In this process you are struggling hard. You are putting a lot of will and effort into that. As long as you succeed you have no problems at all. You cannot always succeed—you know all that.

But there is somehow hope somewhere that it will be possible for you to always succeed. The problem is frustration. The frustration is there because you find that you cannot succeed always—yet there is hope. Whether it is for material goals or spiritual goals, the demand is to succeed in your efforts to reach, attain or accomplish whatever goals you have placed before yourself.

You have to help me. I am not here to give any talk.

I ask the question repeatedly, when people come to see me, a very simple question: you must be very clear as to what you want. "I want this, I don't want that." It's all right. When once you know exactly what you want, you will be able to find out the ways and means of fulfilling your wants. Unfortunately, people want too many things at the same time.

So, you crystallize all of your wants into one basic want, because all the other wants are variations of the same want. You reject my suggestion that man always wants to be happy without even rare moments of unhappiness or permanent pleasure without pain, which, as I said a while ago, is a physical impossibility.

The body cannot take any sensation, be it pleasurable or painful, for long—it is destroying the sensitivity of the sensory perceptions, and also destroying the sensitivity of the nervous system.

Q: *If he is all the time...*

U.G.: If he is all the time concerned about the goals he has, the permanent pleasure. There is a sensation of pleasure. The moment you recognize a particular sensation as a pleasurable sensation, naturally there is a demand to make that pleasurable sensation last longer. So, every sensation, depending upon the intensity of that sensation, which is plagued by you to invest it with more intensity or less intensity, depending upon what you are after, has a limited life of its own.

102

The demand comes only when you separate yourself from that pleasurable sensation and begin to think as to how you can extend the limits of the pleasurable sensation or the moments of happiness. Your thinking has turned that particular demand on your part, to make this particular pleasurable sensation last longer than what the natural duration of its life is, into a problem. Not necessarily your problem, but it has turned that into a problem for the functioning of this body. So it has created a neurological problem and it is trying to absorb that, and doing everything possible to absorb that. Whereas your thinking makes it impossible for this body to handle that in its own way, for the simple reason that you are trying to solve those problems within the field of your religious or psychological approaches.

Actually, those problems are neurological problems, and if the body is left alone to handle them in its own way, it will do a better job than your trying to solve them on psychological or religious levels. All the solutions that we have been offered, given, and the solutions which we have been practicing for centuries, have not done any good except to give us a little bit of comfort, a palliative to bear the pain with some kind of a satisfaction. Yet, you see you are not free from that pain at all. It's because of the hope that somehow the instrument, which is turning all these things into problems, can solve the problems through the same instrument—that is the only thing that this mechanics of thinking can do—that is to create a problem, but it can never, never solve the problem. That is all that I am emphasizing. So if that is not the instrument to solve the problems, is there any other instrument? I say no. It can only create the problems; it cannot solve the problems.

When this understanding dawns on you, then you will realize, in the light of that understanding, that you don't need to use any effort or any will to solve those problems, either on a psychological level or within the framework of your religious thinking. The whole structure slows down, and once it slows down, the energy that is there in the body—which is a manifestation of life or an expression of life—handles things in a tremendously easier way than the frictional thinking, which you are generating through your ideas of how to handle these problems. That's all that I am suggesting.

Q: *So, when you feel that you have a problem you just leave it?*

U.G.: You see, if you put it that way then there is a demand from the person who is suggesting that, to ask how you can leave that alone. You know that you cannot leave it alone—you just say, "Leave it alone." Naturally the next question will be, how to leave that alone without the inter-ference of this thought. There is no "how."

So, if anybody suggests how, you are caught up in the same vicious circle. That is how all these therapists we have in our midst today and all those gurus we have in the marketplace, who are suggesting umpteen numbers of techniques, are creating this tremendous burden which does not in any way lighten the load, but on the other hand, it is adding more and more burden to this situation in which you find yourself today.

So, all those systems and techniques cannot be of any help except that they will act as palliatives for a while so you can bear the pain for a little longer than it is possible for you. That is why you are attracted to this. On the other hand, they are disturbing the whole chemistry of the body, instead of being of any help to you to solve the problems for yourself.

Q: *They are disturbing the chemistry?*

U.G.: They are disturbing the chemistry, and in this process it is throwing up all kinds of aberrations, which you consider to be a sort of spiritual experience. So, your breathing exercises, your yoga exercises, your meditations, are disturbing the chemistry of the body, and the natural rhythm of the body, in exactly the same way that all these drugs which people take disturb the chemistry of the body. So, you say that they are damaging, but actually these are far more damaging than those drugs.

I am not suggesting that you should take drugs, but the purpose of your using the drugs is the same as all these therapies—spiritual or psychological therapies—that all those therapists, religious and psychological, are dishing out day after day after day. The fact that they give you some relief, like Anacin—you have a headache and you don't even give the opportunity for the body to handle it for a little while—so you rush to the market and buy Anacin or aspirin or something and you drug yourself. In exactly the same way it makes it difficult for the body to manufacture the natural things that are there in your body to help relieve you of the pain. It has all the hallucinogens you are talking about as part of its system because it wants to control the pain and relieve itself of the pain. It knows only the physical pain, and it is not interested in your psychological pain at all. The solutions they are offering are only in the area of the psychological field, but not in the physical field.

So, if you take aspirin, for example, it destroys the capacity of this body to handle that pain in a natural way. I am not suggesting that you should take the natural way and switch over to macrobiotics or any other funny health food stuff. That is as vicious and mischievous as any other medicine.

Q: *What then is your clear advice if you have problems? Your advice is not to create them, but if you have psychological...*

U.G.: You cannot but create the problems.

Q: *One of the things I understood is that...*

U.G.: You are creating the problems, number one.

Q: *That's right.*

U.G.: But actually you are not looking at the problems at all. You are not dealing with the problems. You are more interested in solutions than the problems. That makes it difficult for you to look at the problem.

I am suggesting "Look here, you don't have any problems." You assert with all the emphasis at your command, with tremendous animation, "Look, I have a problem here."

All right, you have a problem here. That problem you are talking about is something which you cannot pinpoint and say, "This is the problem." If it is physical pain, it is a reality. So, you go to a doctor; whether it is good for the body or not, whether it is a poison or not, it produces the required relief, however short it may be. But the therapies that those people are dishing out intensify the problem, which is non-existing—the problem is not there any more. You are only searching for the solutions. If there is anything to those solutions that they are offering, the problems should go, should disappear. Actually the problem is still there, but you never question the solutions that those people are offering you as a relief or as something that can free you from the problems.

If you question the solutions that have been offered to us by all those people who are marketing these goodies in the name of holiness, enlightenment, transformation, you will find they are really not the solutions. If they were the solutions, they should produce the results here and free you from the problem. They do not.

You don't question the solutions because the sentiment creeps in there—that fellow who is selling this in the marketplace cannot be a fraud, cannot be a fake. You take him to be an enlightened man or a god walking on the face of the earth. That god may be fooling and kidding himself, may be indulging in self-deception all the time and then selling that stuff, that shoddy piece of goods, to you. You don't question the solutions because then you will be questioning the man who is selling this—his integrity you are questioning—he cannot be dishonest; a holy man cannot be dishonest.

Yet you have to question the solutions because those solutions are not solving your problems. Why don't you question those solutions and put them to the test and test the validity of those solutions? When once you find that they don't work, you have to throw them out, down the drain, out of the window. But you don't do it because of the hope that somehow those solutions will give you the relief that you are after. The instrument, which you are using, is the one that has created this problem. So that instrument will never, never accept the possibility that those solutions are fake solutions. They are not the solutions at all.

The hope keeps you going. That makes it difficult for you to look at the problems. If one solution fails, you go somewhere else and pick up another solution. If that solution fails you go somewhere else and pick another solution. So, you are shopping around with all these solutions but never once will you look at this problem and ask yourself, "What is the problem?"

I don't see any problem. I see only that you are interested in solutions and you come here and ask the same question, "I want another solution." I say, "Those solutions have not helped you at all, so why do you want another solution?" You see it will be the same. You will add one more to your list of solutions, but you will end up in exactly the same way. If you find the uselessness of one, if you see one of them, you have seen them all. You don't have to try one after the other.

What I am suggesting is, if that is the solution you should be free from the problem. If that is not the solution, if there is nothing that you can do about it, even then the problem is not even there. So, you are not interested in solving the problem, because that will put an end to you. You want the problems to remain. You want the hunger to remain because if you are not hungry you will not seek this food from all these holy men. What they are giving you are some scraps, some bits of food, and you are satisfied. Even assuming for a moment that he can give you the whole loaf of bread, which he cannot do (he will only promise or keep it hidden somewhere)—bit by bit, bit by bit he gives you, and thereby you are not dealing with the problem of hunger. You are more interested in getting more crumbs from that fellow, who is promising you, than dealing with your problem of hunger.

Q: *It's like going to a movie, running away from reality.*

U.G.: You never look at the problem. What is the problem? Anger, for example. I don't want to discuss all those silly things, which these people have been discussing for centuries. Anger—where is that anger? Can you separate the anger from the functioning of this body? It's like a wave in the ocean. Can you separate the waves from the ocean? You can sit there and wait until the waves subside, so that you can have a swim in the ocean. Like King Canute (we had to study that little poem) who sat there for years and years hoping that those waves in the ocean would disappear so that he could have a swim in a calm ocean. That will never happen. All right, you can sit there and learn all about how these waves, the high tide and the low tide are caused in the oceans—the scientists have given us all kinds of explanations—but the knowledge about that, the scientific way of explaining those tides, low or high, is not going to be of any help to you.

You are not really dealing with anger at all. Where do you feel the anger, first of all? Where do you feel all these so-called problems you want to be free from? The desires—the burning desires. The desire burns you. Hunger burns you. So, the solutions you have or the means of fulfilling them are very simple and make it impossible for that to burn itself out in your system.

Where do you feel the fear? You feel it here in the pit of your stomach. It is part of the body. The body cannot take those high and low tides of this energy that is there in your body. So your wanting to suppress it for some reason, for some spiritual or social reasons, is not going to succeed.

Actually you are not dealing with anger. Anger is energy; it's a tremendous outburst of energy. And by destroying that energy through any means, you are destroying the very expression of life itself. It becomes a problem only when you try to do something with that energy. When once it is absorbed by the system, you will not do the things that you think you will do if the anger is left alone. You are actually not dealing with the anger, but the frustration. Or, to avoid such a situation which has resulted in clumsiness in your relationships or in your understanding of yourself so that it should not appear again. In the future, you are interested, but this time you have not succeeded in doing anything with the anger, so you want to be prepared to meet such situations as and when they arise in the future.

The instrument, which you are using, has been used by you so far all these times, every time there is an outburst of anger you have used this, yet you have not succeeded in freeing yourself from the anger. So you don't have any extraordinary instrument, you won't come into the position of anything extraordinary, other than this instrument which you have been using all these years, and at the same time you hope that somehow this very thing will help you to be free from the anger tomorrow. It is the same hope.

Q: *But if somebody is very angry, he or she may become violent.*

U.G.: Yes. The violence is absorbed by the body.

Q: *And threatening.*

U.G.: To whom?

Q: *To other people.*

U.G.: Yes. So? So what?

Q: *Running around with a knife.*

U.G.: All right, so what?

Q: *Killing somebody else.*

U.G.: Yes. Why are you killing people, thousands of people, for no fault of theirs? Why are you limiting something which is natural there, but why are you not condemning the nations that are dropping these cluster bombs on helpless people? Do you call them sane? Why are you condemning this particular thing? You see both of them have sprung from the same source. As long as you do anything to control your anger here, so long will you indulge in such atrocious things and justify them, because that is the only way to protect your way of life and your way of thinking. These two things go together. Why do you justify that? That is insane—through no fault of theirs.

He is not hurting you, but he is disturbing your way of

life, there is a danger of that man taking away everything that you consider to be your precious things. This idea of stopping this man from acting when there is an outburst of anger is exactly the same.

The religious man has found that an angry man will be an anti-social man. As long as he practices virtues, so long he will remain an anti-social man, and he will act out of anger. When that goal that the society has placed before you, that same goal which you have accepted for yourself as an ideal goal to be practiced, is finished for you, you will not harm anybody, either individually or collectively as a nation.

You have to deal with the anger. You are dealing with something totally unrelated to the anger; not even once do you let that anger burn itself out within the framework of where it originates and functions. Having some therapy of hitting your pillows, hitting this, that, and the other, is just a joke. That does not free the man from the anger once and for all.

Q: *Hitting on a pillow?*

U.G.: That's what they do, one of the therapies they have …

Q: *It doesn't help?*

U.G.: It will appear again. You take it out on something, the pillow, whether you take it out on the pillow or on somebody else, your neighbor or your husband or wife as the case may be—he can take it in the name of love, that's a different matter—but if you try it on your boss, you have had it. You will be out of your job.

So what do you do? That is the goal which you have placed before yourself. So you are not dealing with anger, you will never deal with this anger at all as long as you are interested in finding out a way of not hitting the person who is coming at you with a knife. You have to protect yourself; I am not for a moment saying not to protect yourself. Instead of that, you are using anger as a shield, which is making it impossible for you to physically protect yourself, that is essential. Your anger makes it impossible for you to deal with that situation. Don't say that it's non-violence or you should not hurt somebody else—he is hurting you. Even in the Bible, it is an eye for an eye, a tooth for a tooth. You never practice that. Of course, they practice it on a larger scale, but in daily life it is something terrible to do.

I don't see any problem at all. I don't see any problem. Nobody wants to look at the problem for the simple reason he is more interested in solutions rather than the problem. What is the problem?

There is no point in discussing those hypothetical situations for the simple reason that the person who is hopping mad with anger, burning with anger, will not sit and discuss the question of anger. That is amazing. That's the time to deal with those things, when you are really burning with anger, burning with desire, burning with all those things that you want to be free from. Otherwise, it becomes a classroom discussion—somebody talking on the anatomy of anger, the anatomy of how the anger arises, or the anatomy of love. It's too ridiculous. Or, they offer solutions, which don't work when there is really a situation like that. That's the reason why I don't discuss all these things.

No problem. There's no problem for the individual. When he's mad with anger—that's the time for him to deal with it. So where is the time for him to do it? He cannot do two things together, you see, it stops the thinking. Do you think that man will act in a thoughtless way? He will act in a thoughtless way because you are not dealing with the anger at that moment, but how not to, or how to prevent the results of letting that anger stay there. So it is that that is responsible for beating or doing something but actually not when the anger is burning the whole of your being.

Long silence.

U.G.: Sorry, we are stuck again.

Q: *U.G.?*

U.G.: Yes sir?

Q.: *Is there a possibility of looking at the problem?*

U.G.: No, because you are yourself the problem.

Q: *So, there is no answer?*

U.G.: There is no way of separating yourself from the problem. That's what you are trying. That is what I mean by saying that you are putting anger out there and trying to look and deal with it as if it is an object outside of you or it is something outside of you. When you separate yourself, the only action is what you fear would happen. That is inevitable. So you have no way of controlling that at all. Is there anything that you can do to prevent this separation from what you are? It is a horrible thing to realize that you are yourself anger and whatever you do to stop that, prevent it, or do something about it, is false. That will be tomorrow or in your next life—not now.

So that is what you are; you are not a spiritual man or a religious man. You can imagine that you are a religious man, because you are trying to control your anger, or trying to be free from anger, or trying to be less and less angry as the years go by. All that makes you feel that you are not that vicious man whom you avoid. You are no different. You are not any more spiritual than the people whom you condemn.

Tomorrow you are going to be a marvelous person; you will be free from anger. What do you want me to do in the meantime? Admire you because you have put on the label that you are a spiritual man or that you have put on fancy robes? What do you want me to do? For that you want me to admire you? There is nothing there to be admired because you are as vicious as anybody else in this world. Condemning that has no meaning, or adopting a posture, which is totally unrelated to what is happening there, has no meaning either.

So, how can you put on this posture or adopt some kind of an attitude and feel superior to the animals? The animals are better than the humans. If there is anger, the animal acts and that is only for the purpose of survival, you understand, only for survival! If you kill your fellow man for feeding yourself that is a moral act—only for that purpose, because if you look around, one form of life lives on another form of life.

And if you talk of vegetarianism and kill millions of people, that is the most immoral, unpardonable act that a civilized culture of human beings can ever do. Do you see the absurdity of the two? You condemn this and you love the animals. What for do you love the animals? What about the human beings there, you are murdering, massacring, simply because they are a threat to you? They are one day going to take away everything that you have. So, in anticipation of those people coming and robbing everything you think you have a right to, so you want to prevent the possibility by massacring them in the name of a belief, in the name of God knows what. That is what religions have done right from the beginning.

So, what is the point in reviving all those religions? What is the point in all those hosts of gurus coming into these countries preaching something that does not operate in their own lives or in the countries they come from? They

; of life and unity of life all the time, but
in their lives. What does it mean? You
ble thing that is a necessity for your sur-
moral action. Not to survive, not to feed
f perversion.
: foundation on which the whole Christian
don't forget that. You suffer in the hope
inent seat there in heaven—non-existing
ing through hell now in the hope of reach-
ur death. What for? So suffer.
mphasize that. Bear the pain; the endur-
ance of pain is the means. You go through hell in the hope of
having paradise at the end of your life, or the end of a series
of lives if you want to believe that. I am just pointing out
the absurdity of talking about these things. The religious
things have really no meaning—when you are pushed into
a corner, you will behave exactly like anybody else. So this
culture, your values, religious or otherwise, hasn't touched
a bit there.

If man is freed from this moral dilemma, which has
been the basis of the whole thinking of man, then he will
live like a human being—not a spiritual man, not a religious
man. A religious man is no good for the society. A kind man
is a menace to the society—one who is practicing kindness
as a fine art.

Q: ...is a menace?

U.G.: ...is a menace to the society because all the destruction has come out of that—one who talked of love, one who
talked of "Love thy neighbor as thyself," one who talked of
non-violence. All the destructive forces originated in the
thinking of that man. So, we are all the inheritors of that
culture. We cannot do anything but that.

You are freed from the burden of this, the falseness

of the whole culture. Individually you are freed from the totality of all the absurdities that have been imposed on us. That's all that I am saying.

Q: *I can't really accept...*
U.G.: You can't accept, I know.

Q: *No I can't accept that there are persons, for instance, Jesus, not Christianity, not the church, who are real people.*

U.G.: Why did they put him on the cross and nail him to death?

Q: *People did. They made a god of man. I don't agree with that.*

U.G.: Not even an ordinary man, because he made statements out of which the whole dogmatic teaching of Christianity originated. Certainly. That applies to every teacher. I am not condemning only Jesus. All teachers—Buddha, Mohammed and Mahavi—all the teachers whom we consider to be the great religious teachers of mankind, let alone those people who are doing holy business in the marketplace today. We are not concerned about this. There is no use blaming them anyway.

So, we are here. We are the inheritors of all that violent culture. So, your culture is nothing but to teach man how to kill and to be killed, whether it is in the name of religion or in the name of political ideology, or in the name of patriotism, or anything you want. It can't be anything different. That is why I said that the whole thing is moving in the direction of the total annihilation of man. We have set such things in motion—forces of destruction, which no power can stop.

Q: *Yes. No power.*

U.G.: No power, no god can stop it because those gods themselves have set in motion these forces of destruction. You see that now happening. When the caveman used the jawbone of an ass to kill his neighbor, there were chances of survival for others. The same cave man today, who lives there in the Kremlin and in the White House, and in the Parliament House there in India—are the ones who will set in motion, who will let loose forces of destruction that will completely wipe out every form of life on this planet, and man will take with him every species that exists today on this planet. It has all come out of that thinking of man who taught religion to man, who wanted to establish love on the face of this earth—and see what he has made out of it!

Q: *So, if you say we can't stop it…*

U.G.: Can you? Can you stop it? You can't stop it. So the one thing that you can do is to …

Q: *I think that as humanity we can stop it if we want to.*

U.G.: When?

Q.: *If we want it.*

U.G.: Well you don't want to obviously. Do you want?

Q: *Yes.*

U.G.: Then how do you go about it? How do you go about it—tell me. Do you see the urgency of the whole situation? Some lunatic there may press the button. So, we sit here comfortably and talk about these things …

Q: *I think there is a possibility that we can stop it.*

117

U.G.: What is the possibility?

Q: *To stop it.*

U.G.: What is the possibility?

Q: *To act.*

U.G.: How? When are you going to act? When the time is too late. When the whole thing, the holocaust, is released, it will be too late. Or, you can join the anti-bomb movement—which is ridiculous.

Q: *It's ridiculous?*

U.G.: Yes, of course.

Q: *It's too late?*

U.G.: Don't you want the police to protect your tiny little property? The hydrogen bomb is an extension of the same. You can't say, "This I want, and that I don't want." It is an extension of the same.

Q: *So, we are helpless?*

U.G.: No. What makes you think that it is possible for you to stop this? You can stop it in you. Free yourself from that social structure that is operating in you without becoming anti-social, without becoming a reformer, without becoming anti-this, anti-that. You can throw the whole thing out of your system and free yourself from the burden of this culture, for yourself and by yourself. Whether it has any use for the society or not is not your concern. If there is one individual who walks free, you don't have any more the choking feeling of what this horrible culture has done to you. It's neither East nor West; it's all the same. Human nature is exactly the same—there's no difference.

You are interested only in what to do, what to do.

Q: *We all are.*

U.G.: How can we stop? Individually there isn't a damn thing that you can do. Collectively you can create a Salvation Army, like that. That's all. So what—another church, another Bible, another preacher?

After a long silence...

Q1: *What do you think about such an answer?*

Q2: *The words came "speechless."*

Q3: *What do I think about such an answer? I do agree, but it's very theoretical. Just free yourself of the burden of culture. I understand it. But practically it's very difficult, of course. There's almost nothing I can do about it.*

U.G.: There is nothing, not a thing.

Q3: *You are a product of that.*

U.G.: You have no freedom of action at all.

Q: *No.*

U.G.: When that is understood, what is there expresses itself. The intelligence that is there, which is the result of millions and millions and millions of years of the creative nature, can handle things much more effectively than all the solutions that man has come out with through his thinking. That's all. The ideal that we have placed before us, the perfect man, is just a myth. Such a man doesn't exist at all.

Q: *The ideal man?*

U.G.: The ideal man doesn't exist. It is just a word, an idea. All your life you are trying to become that ideal man and what you are left with is the misery, the suffering. To be that some day, that's the hope. We will die with that hope.

Q: *So, one solution is to accept your being here, as you are.*

U.G.: As you are, exactly the way you are. Then you are not in conflict with society. You see the demand that is pushing you in the direction of wanting to change yourself into something—that is what the culture has done, has put in you. If you want to do something—"Boy, look here, watch your step." That is what they are doing.

The second movement that comes, that is the society. "Watch your step," it says. So, that has put fear in you. Then at the same time it talks of freeing yourself from fear, and courage and the whole thing—be a fearless man—that is only for the purpose of using you as a pawn in maintaining the status quo of the society.

That is why it is teaching courage, it is teaching fearlessness, so that it can use you to maintain the continuity of the society. You are a part of that. That is why every time you want to act, what is there is fear and the impossibility of acting. The society and the culture are not "out there." Unless you are free from that you cannot act.

Q: *Unless, and then you are free from it? Then you can act.*

U.G.: Then you will not come here and ask me the question,

"What will be that action?"

Q: *No I don't ask that. Then you act.*

U.G.: There is an action already. There is an action as far as you are concerned.

Q: *So, you mean that the man is only entitled to act when he is free from society.*

U.G.: He is not able to act, because he is all the time thinking in terms of the freedom to act. "How can I be free to act?" That's all that you are concerned about, the freedom. But you are not acting—that freedom, the demand for the freedom to act is preventing the action, which is neither social nor anti-social.

Q: *So, you are free if you accept yourself and your situation?*

U.G.: That's all. You are not in conflict with the society any more. That's the reality of the world. Whether you will be of any use to the society or not—you will not be any use to the society. On the other hand, if you become a threat to the society, the society will liquidate you, because it is disturbing all the movements in the direction of the status quo. That's all.

You are a neurotic because you want two things at the same time. It is that that has created this problem for you—wanting two things at the same time. You want to bring about a change in you—that change is the demand of the society so that you can become a part of that and maintain the continuity of the social structure without any change. This is the conflict.

When the demand for bringing about any change in you ceases, then the concern to change the world around you also comes to an end, *ipso facto*—both of them are finished. Otherwise, your actions will be a danger to the society. They will liquidate you, that's for sure. So, you are ready to be liquidated by that social structure—that is the courage.

Not to die in the battlefields, to fight for your flag. What does a flag symbolize? You wave your flag here, they wave their flag, and then both of them talk of peace. How absurd the whole situation is. And yet you talk of peace. You owe allegiance to your flag and they owe allegiance to their flag, and you are at the same time talking of peace in this world? How can there be any peace in this world when you are waving your flag here, and they are waving their flag? Whoever has better weapons will have the day for himself. With my flag here, your flag there—these peace marchers—or you create another flag with the anti-bomb groups.

Q: *It's useless.*

U.G.: I don't have to tell you. Are you ready to do away with the policeman? Individually, you want to protect yourself, your life number one—I am not saying whether you should or should not—or your little property you have. So, you need the help of the policeman to protect it. So you draw a line and say, "This is my nation," so you see, you want to protect your nation. The frontiers are expanding, and, when you cannot do it, you will have to expand your means of destruction also to protect yourself, and you will say it is defensive. Certainly it is defensive. That is only an extension of this. You can't talk against that as long as you want this policeman to protect your things. You can sit around there, go on marches, sit around those nuclear reactors, sing peace songs and play guitars, and "make love, not war"—don't listen to all that crap—making love and making war spring from the same source. That becomes a sham mockery in these people.

That's enough I think. That's enough.

* * * * * * *

Q: *So what then is this relationship between ourselves and the world we live in?*

U.G.: Absolutely nothing except that the world you experience is the one that is created by you. You are living in a world of your own. You have created a world of your own experiences and you are trying to project it on the world. You have no way of experiencing the reality of the world at all. You and I use the same word to describe that as a video camera. What you are holding as a pen, or a pencil, as the case may be. So, we have to accept all these things as valid because they are workable, they make us function in this world, to communicate only on that level intelligently.

Q: *So nobody can be an example for anybody else?*

U.G.: It's only for the animals. Not for the humans. A human being cannot follow anybody. Physically you have to depend; but that is all there is to it.

Q: *Would you say that there is no such thing as growth in spirituality?*

U.G.: What I am suggesting is that there is no such thing as spirituality at all. If you superimpose what you call spirituality on what is called material life, then you create problems for yourself, because you see growth—birth, growth and development in the material world around you. So, you are applying that to this so-called spiritual life also.

Q: *Do you suggest that the problem starts when you start separating things?*

U.G.: Separating things, dividing things into two—material life, and spiritual life—but there is only one life. This is a material life, and that other has no relevance. Wanting to adjust your material life or to change your material life into that so-called religious pattern given to you, placed before you by these religious people, is destroying the possibility of your living in harmony and accepting the reality of this material world exactly the way it is. It is that which is responsible for your pain, for your suffering, for your sorrow.

There is a constant struggle on your part to be like that, you see, and to chase something that does not exist, and has no meaning at all. That gives you some feeling that the doing is all that is important for you, not the actual achievement of that. It is moving farther and farther away. The more effort you put into it, the more you feel good. Like the problems you have—trying to solve the problems is all that is important to you, but the solutions are more interesting to you than the problems. You are more interested in solutions than looking at the problem. What is the problem, I say. You have no problems; you have only solutions. What is the problem? Nobody tells me what the problem is.

You are telling me that these are all the solutions. Which one should I use to solve my problem? What exactly is the problem?

The material problems are understandable. If you don't have health, you have to do something about your health. If you don't have money, you have to do something about money. These are understandable. If you have some psychological problems, there the real problem begins. All these psychologists and the religious people with their therapies and their solutions are trying to help you, but they don't lead you anywhere, do they? No, the individuals remain as shallow and as empty as ever before. What do they want to prove to themselves?

Q: *You believe that problems solve themselves by going along with your own life?*

U.G.: What is the problem? You never look at the problem. It is not possible for you to look at the problem as long as you are interested in the solutions.

Q: *But don't you want solutions?*

U.G.: You are only interested in solutions, not in solving the problem.

Q: *Isn't that the same thing then?*

U.G.: In that process, you find out that those solutions are really worthless—those solutions don't solve your problem, whatever is the problem. Those solutions keep the problems going. They don't solve them. If there is something wrong with your tape recorder, or your television, that can be remedied. There is a technician who can help you. But this is an endless process going on and on and on and on, all your life—more and more of something and less and less of the other.

So, you never question the solutions. If you really question the solutions, you will end up in that process questioning the persons who have offered you those solutions. Then sentimentality comes in the way of your rejecting not only the solutions, but those persons who have offered you the solutions. That requires a tremendous courage on your part.

You can have the courage to climb the mountain, swim the lakes and go on a raft to the other side of the Atlantic or Pacific. That any fool can do. But the courage to be on your own, to stand on your two solid feet, is something which cannot be given by somebody. If you are freed from the burden of the entire past of mankind, then what is there is the courage.

Epilogue

by Ellen Chrystal

When U.G. was having these conversations in Amsterdam in 1982, I was living in California in the spiritual community of Da Free John (Adi Da). In 1985 I left the guru and found myself, after 10 years of practice in that community, out on my ass—no money, no home, no relationship to family and friends.

I was beginning to sense that all of my effort and striving to find spiritual enlightenment was somehow false—an imposition on the simplicity of being. Yet seeking was such a habit, I had developed such a strong identity as a spiritual aspirant, and there was still that burning question: what the hell *is* this?

U.G. says that his "calamity" which occurred in 1967 on his 49th birthday was a flushing out of everything that every man, woman and child ever thought felt or experienced—or as he liked to say, "The saints went marching out." What he is saying goes against everything we have been taught by the culture—religious, philosophical, psychological and even scientific. We really can't or don't want to hear this, and so we continually try to put him into a framework that we can use to form concepts about him. We really can't help ourselves, but he did his best to undermine this.

U.G. once asked me what I learned during my time with Adi Da. It was a strange question coming from U.G., but without hesitation I told him that I learned to type. He was sincerely impressed. For him there was no spiritual or material, but we should be able to function sanely and intelligently in this world, make a living and stand on our own two feet, and typing was, after all, a useful skill. It served me well for many years as I worked in New York City for the partner of a major law firm.

It was while I was at this job that I had the idea of transcribing the audiotapes of the conversations that comprise this book. I was very drawn to these conversations, which seemed to be a lively composite of U.G.'s fundamental expression. My original thought was that perhaps by transcribing the tapes, I might imbibe U.G.'s understanding in some way—I wish it was that easy. So, in between dictation, preparing legal briefs, filing, scheduling and answering phone calls, I stuck the cassette tapes called "Give Up" into my transcribing machine and typed away.

The first time I became aware of U.G. was about two years after I left Adi Da. In 1987, I went on a three-day retreat with Bernadette Roberts (an ex-Carmelite nun, who claims to be in a state of "no self"). During the retreat, I was thoroughly refreshed by Bernadette's down-to-earth wisdom, simplicity and humor. As the retreat was nearing its end, an old friend of mine (another "divorcée," as U.G. calls those who have left their gurus) was handing a book to Bernadette called "*The Mystique of Enlightenment, Conversations with U.G. Krishnamurti.*" Bernadette gave the book back to my friend, and I quickly said, "If you don't mind, I would like to read that."

With the book in hand, I withdrew to my cabin. The first thing I noticed was U.G.'s droll disclaimer at the beginning of the book: "*This book has no copyright...*" This very statement was quite exhilarating after having spent the past ten years with a man who claimed a perpetual copyright on every word he uttered.

During the last few hours of the retreat I read the book from cover-to-cover. I was reading the truth that I had always sensed on an intuitive level, and it left me feeling clear and unburdened. It was the beginning of the unraveling of my search.

The book had been published in India. I wrote to the publisher, inquiring about U.G.'s whereabouts and whether I could meet him. After several months, I received a letter from a man named Chandrasekhar—U.G. was traveling; I could contact Julie Thayer, who just happened to live a few blocks from me on the upper West side of Manhattan!

I called Julie and she kindly invited me over to her apartment, and I immediately ran over there. Julie was a photographer who had just completed a round-the-world trip with U.G. and had taken video footage of him everywhere they went. There were about 100 hours of unedited tapes. For several weeks I went to Julie's apartment every day and sat mesmerized, watching video footage of this odd man as he wandered around the world, meeting and conversing with an eclectic assortment of people. Soon after that, U.G. came to the United States and I flew to San Rafael, California, to meet him for the first time.

"Why have you wasted your money?" he asked me as soon as I walked in the door. "I wanted to meet you," I answered. "Well, you won't get anything here," he told me, adding, "If you got anything at all from those books you wouldn't be here." I just sat down and smiled. What could I say? Something was going on, but it was certainly nothing I could understand, explain or make use of. I had no frame of reference for this guy. All my guru-worship lessons from the past were of no use here. But, at the same time, he was clearly no ordinary man, and I became irretrievably linked to him.

All I could do when I first met U.G. was to observe how he functioned. After years of bowing and scraping at the feet of Da Free John, it was quite refreshing to sit around with someone, who seemed to me to be in a state I would call "enlightened" (a term U.G. would never use), and not have to perform any ceremony or make any effort to express anything in particular. There was absolutely no "stink of enlightenment." I could just be there and be myself.

However, I must admit that I still had some residue of seeking, which is like a drug, and I was an addict who would occasionally fall off the wagon. U.G. would often say, "What brings you here, will take you somewhere else."

One day when U.G. was visiting New York, I told him that I was going to return to the community of Adi Da. He showed no reaction other than to say, "Of course, you won't get anything here." And then, "But you won't get anything there either." He was correct. After a few months of revisiting Adi Da, I guess I washed that man right out of my hair and he never returned.

The next time I saw U.G., he didn't even mention my dalliance. I just walked in the door, said, "Hi U.G., it's great to see you!" and sat down. I never had any sense with U.G. that he expected or wanted me to be there, or not be there. He was there. Take it or leave it. Although in his lovely way he would always tell me, "Madam, you are always welcome."

Although U.G. criticized the spiritual marketplace, and blasted all that the culture has placed before us as an ideal, especially as imposed on us by religion, he had no problem one way or the other with people taking on a religion or practice. He never discouraged or encouraged. If that was what was real for you, then do it. It's just that it was not real for me, and so at some point, it fell away.

In 2004, I was visiting U.G. in Gstaad where he had recently come up with his "108 Money Maxims," which was a list of 108 very politically incorrect sayings about money. A friend had created a deck of 108 cards, with each card presenting a particular money maxim. They were quite funny and slightly shocking, especially because money is often such a confusing and anxiety-producing issue for spiritual seekers. Here I would like to point out that U.G. never required anyone to give him money to see him. He also made no money from his books. Yet, money flowed in and out of his hands like the waters of life.

One day U.G. asked me to pick a card from the Money Maxims. I did so, and as he read it to me, he looked at me with his most mischievous expression, which he had developed fully in his later years, and read, *"TAKE THE DOUGH AND HIT THE ROAD."* The seed was planted. Within the year I took early retirement, sold my NYC apartment for three times what I paid for it, got rid of all my possessions, except what I could fit into my 1988 Toyota Land Cruiser and headed for Palm Springs where U.G. was visiting at the time. When I arrived in Palm Springs I asked him if I could travel with him and he said yes. So I took the dough and hit the road with U.G.!

U.G. was famous for his constant travels. He had no fixed abode, he owned nothing, wherever he went he would stay in a rented place or friends would accommodate him, but he always made sure not to put people out, and would never inconvenience anyone. Everything was done with a kind of spontaneous rhythm, with no room for drama, just function. Get along or get out.

So many people would come to see him, and especially in India, the people would be packed like sardines sitting on the floor or chairs inside, hovering around the doorway and windows—everyone was welcome without formality. It was amazing to see the grace and kindness he showed to the people coming to see him. He had an ability to sit for hours on end relating to people collectively and individually. He was so humorous, clear and direct with each person—there was a liberating freedom in his company. There also seemed to be a gravitational pull—people would be drawn into his field for a time and whatever the influence—being around him did not require any conditions, do's or don'ts. You were

131

in the fire and it could be warm and cozy or burning like hell.

He traveled the world with his little suitcase in hand, visiting with people everywhere he went. Not giving lectures or selling books, but simply sitting in a room somewhere while people came and went. Some people were not interested in what he had to say, and that was fine with him, because he really did not believe he had any mission at all. Others would hang on every word of his, and those he would constantly confront and confound. Others would come for a visit and then never return, which was also fine with him. His door was always open to anyone and everyone without conditions or expectations.

By the time I was traveling with U.G., he was already in his late 80's, and yet rather than slow down, he was more and more animated and had larger groups of people around him all the time. There was no organization yet there was some kind of natural structure to the days. At the same time, there was always the sudden, unpredictable movement from place to place, with long rides in cars to strange destinations.

In the earlier days when I first met U.G., his drives, which he called his "constitutionals," were his way taking a break from the people, but now he was taking us all along, in caravans of cars stuffed to the brim with bodies. Stopping at gas stations to relieve ourselves and buy junk food to eat in the car.

On other days he would just sit in a room, with anyone and everyone who was there, sitting for hours and hours—the entire room suddenly falling asleep (one young girl coined the phrase "spiritual coma" to describe this phenomenon), checking emails, or just "eyeballing" U.G. from early morning hours until the sun went down. Sometimes there would be spontaneous revelries and entertainment, which could get quite wild and cause a bit of consternation amongst those looking for deep philosophical conversation and spiritual guidance.

At this point, people were also eating all their meals around U.G. In the earlier days, meals would be a time for people to go off on their own, while U.G. would eat his simple meal alone or with a few friends. Now, it became a moveable feast for whoever happened to be there, and there were many. And yet, the miracle of this was that there was absolutely no formal control or organization—it was the action of anarchy—breakfast, lunch, dinner and "high tea," full meals were served four times a day—I got fat and everyone else stayed slim and trim. The food was bought, meals prepared and served, the table cleared, the kitchen cleaned, and all without any organization or anyone running it. It just worked.

U.G. would only eat a small bowl of iddli or rice sticks, and then immediately throw it out of his system—due to his "plumbing problem."

On March 23, 2007, I received a call from a friend that U.G. had died. I was in Gstaad at the time waiting for him. The words that came forth from deep inside me were "Sat Guru, true guru" and I understood then what U.G. was—the one who gives you nothing but turns you to face the truth without anything or anyone to hold on to.

A few months after U.G.'s death I had a very vivid dream. I walked into a room, which seemed like the stone turret of a castle, and U.G. was standing in the middle of the room. I walked up to him and looked directly into his eyes. I was happy and amazed to see him alive. "You are here," I said to him. Then it became crystal clear to me, and I said, "So, there is no death." He just smiled, walked to the window, morphed into a white bird, and flew away.

Thanks, U.G.

U.G. never wrote a book. All the books we have are transcriptions of his conversations with friends, but he always insisted that the books of his conversations should have no copyright. Thus, this book and others have been reprinted in India, and other countries, and translated into many languages—all freely and without copyright. I am particularly grateful to have the opportunity to edit and reprint this book through Non-Duality Press. I can't express how much it means to me to have Julie Thayer's beautiful photographs of U.G., which grace the front and back cover of this book. Those two pictures alone tell more about U.G. than all the words in this book. My thanks to Louis Brawley for initiating this project, and for making U.G. laugh so much, and my deepest appreciation to my friend Sabyasachi Guha who helps keep U.G. very much alive for me.